AT THE CLIFFS OF ABANDONMENT

ALICIA WHITE

Manufactured in the United States of America

10 9 8 7 6 5 4 3 2 1

Library of Congress Cataloging-in-Publication Data is available.

ISBN: 979-8-89041-324-6

E-ISBN: 979-8-89041-325-3

Hope Noelle White

December 28, 2002–January 29, 2020

DEDICATION

I dedicate this book to our sweet and beautiful, forever seventeen, Hope Noelle. Every moment with you, every touch, every sound of laughter, every heart-filled conversation, every prayer, every family worship time, every special event or occasion, and every opportunity to be your mom transformed me. You have taught me to let go and laugh more. You have taught me to give more. You have taught me to be present in the moment more. You have taught me to love bigger, to love better, and to love deeper. You have taught me to keep my eyes fixed on the kingdom perspective. I am forever grateful the Father allowed us to steward His daughter for a time here on earth. There are not enough words in the universe to describe my love for you and how much I wish I could pour it out upon you still. Your life on earth ended too soon. But until I lock eyes upon you in eternity, I will find my sweet Hope in the forward.

I promise I will take all the "should haves" and "could haves" to be transformed into a better mom, wife, and woman of God. I promise I will be your voice to bring Hope to the hopeless.

Hopie, you are beautiful.

Endorsements

Losing my beloved son, Christian Matthew, in 2019 left a wound that only the Holy Spirit can heal. In the midst of such devastation and, at times, paralyzing grief, this book took me to the depths I needed to go to feel understood. Suicide grief is so very isolating, and there are so few resources for the born-again believer for this heartbreaking experience. Alicia tells it raw and real. Her very words can be felt. If you have lost a child in this manner or know someone who has, please read this book. It will give you Hope to carry on in this painful journey because that Hope comes from our Lord and Savior, Jesus Christ. I am so grateful the Holy Spirit brought this book into my life and inspired and gave Alicia strength to write it.

—Christy Connaughton

As I started reading this book, I found myself saying to the Lord, "Please, Jesus, never put me through this, the pain is too unbearable." Over and over, I found myself weeping for the sorrow that this mother went through. Then I found myself weeping for the depth of care and love she found in her Heavenly Father. I felt like I entered a sacred place between father and daughter. I find myself reading and rereading in search of understanding this depth of God's wisdom. Most of us will never experience the truths that this mom found as she makes her way through layer after layer of excruciating grief. This book is absolutely necessary for this generation. May I tell you that Alicia White is my friend, and, in many ways, she and her family are still finding their way. But she knows that her life and wholeness are found at the cliffs of abandonment. Her Hope is found there also.

—Beth Ritter

TABLE OF CONTENTS

seventeen-year-old, told us not to get involved and that she could handle it herself. But after she left the room, we discussed further our concerns about what had just happened. Jason and I agreed that I would call the store the next day despite her wishes that we would not. Although she was a young lady and almost an adult, we still desired to protect her and keep her safe.

News reports of sex slaves being rescued from all over the United States started to run through my mind. I decided to text a prayer warrior and one of my closest friends, Cindy, who lived in Fort Worth, Texas, to ask for prayer concerning the situation. After she reassured me that she would pray, I texted her back a declaration that Satan couldn't have my girls!

I was not about to let our Hope become a victim of a kidnapping and God knows what else. I realize some might think I was really overreacting, and maybe I was, but fear is not an emotion I normally was subject to, so at the time, I was discerning that God was stirring up in me a warrior spirit to hedge up for my daughter, that no weapon formed against her would prosper. I slept in peace for the rest of the night. I had no idea what the next day would bring.

January 29, 2020, I had an eye appointment that morning, and on my way, I called Kroger to follow through with what Jason and I discussed last night. The manager assured me that if he came back into the store, they would call the police. After my eye appointment, I went to Walmart looking for a Mace keychain to give Hope. Her older sister, Faithanna, had one, but she did not. I thought it would be wise for her to have it just in case. I could not find them at Walmart, so I texted my son, Samuel, in Dallas to ask him and tell him what happened. Not able to find one at Walmart, I decided to go to Lowe's.

While at Lowe's, Cindy, my friend from Ft. Worth, calls me and offers to pray for Hope and the situation over the phone. We again canceled every assignment of the enemy and declared peace and safety for Hope. I continued to look for the pepper spray with no luck. I found Hope and Faithanna ready to go to lunch when I got home. It was Wednesday, and every Wednesday for the past six months or so, Hope and I had made it our lunch date day. She was doing online schooling, so it was just me and her usually at home during the day, so it had enabled us to spend more time together. I cherished our lunch dates. On this particular day, Faithanna, who had just started college, was home and was going with us.

When it was just Hope, she usually drove us in her car. She loved Michael Bublé. We would get in the car, and she would ask me if I wanted to listen to her "boyfriend." She would sing so effortlessly with him. She had a beautiful tone. But on this day, January 29, 2020, we took the van, and I drove both my girls to our usual place. It was China Wok inside our local mall. Except that on that day, they were closed. They had been closed for the last couple of weeks, and as news about the China virus, COVID-19, was just coming out, I remember discussing that day at lunch that the owners probably went back to China for their New Year's and got stuck and could not come back. Little did we know at the time how that virus was going to shift our very culture in America and affect everyone and every place.

So, we each picked out what we wanted to eat that day from the mall food court. As Faithanna was still getting her lunch, Hope and I sat down to eat. She said, out of the blue, a name she wanted for one of her children in the future. I asked her to repeat it because I did not catch it and wanted to remember it, but she got mad that I did not hear her the first time. Faithanna came over to the table with her food and heard the end of the conversation. She encouraged her to tell me again, but Hope refused. I believe this is the moment Satan began to plant the seed for what was to come that day. I could discern she felt rejected, ignored, and not important at that moment—which was further from the truth. She was good at putting up walls when she felt hurt in any way. The enemy had been spoon-feeding her lies for many years. No, this was not the first time Satan perverted our conversations in her head… but that day would be the last. The conversation went on to other things, and we were all laughing by the end of our lunch together.

As we left the mall, Hope wanted a coffee from Starbucks, and there was one inside a Kroger around the corner (not the same one she worked at). The girls went with me to the bank inside the store, and then we went to the Starbucks. When we got back into the car, Faithanna realized she needed some school supplies and went back in. While Hope and I were in the car by ourselves, I decided to tell her about making the phone call to her manager that day. I figured I did not want her going back to work and someone telling her, "Your mom called us." I wanted her to hear it from me. She took it as I thought she would: mad that we got involved. She began to vent in anger. She said she would feel embarrassed to go back to work knowing I called. Now, from an adult's point of view, we know that any good parent would have done the same, and there was nothing to be embarrassed about. But for a low self-esteem seventeen-year-old, who felt like she could handle everything on her own, this was a real emotion. I tried to reason with her, but when Hope became mad, there was no reasoning with her. Satan simply twisted everything you tried to say to her mind. I had learned years ago that when our conversation becomes this heated, the best thing for me to do is to leave her alone, let her vent, and come back to her when she is calmer. These are the last words I said to her: "When you have kids someday, you will understand that I did it out of love for you."

Silenced filled the car. We got home. I unlocked the door. Hope went upstairs to her room—I assumed to do schoolwork. I went down to the basement and sat at my computer to work on a writing for ministry entitled *A Friend of God*. With tears rolling down my face over the words that spewed out of her mouth just a few minutes ago, "I will never trust you again," and "You think we have a good relationship now, but we don't," I tried to refocus on my work. Faithanna, after a few minutes, came down and sat on the stairs and asked me what I was doing. I told her I was just trying to work on ministry stuff. She then came all the way down and lay on Samuel's bed. His room had been in the basement, and although he had gotten married that summer and moved to Dallas, we were keeping his bed up for when they visited. She fell asleep as I tried to type.

After some time, I heard the bathroom door close that was up two floors where our bedrooms were. It had to be Hope going to the restroom. I kept trying to focus, but my mind was on my daughter. After another time had passed, I felt a cool breeze come into the room. It was the basement and winter, so I did not think it was strange to be a bit chilly. I decided to go get a sweater from my room. I noticed, as I was starting back downstairs, that the bathroom door in the hallway was still closed. I knew Hope must have been in there still. I hesitated to go back downstairs and thought maybe I should knock on the door and tell her I love her. I felt an uneasiness in my stomach and deep sadness for how our conversation had ended. But I noticed the sound of the faucet running, so I thought she must be washing her hands. "She is okay," I decided, trying to push off the feeling I was having. I reasoned with myself to wait a bit longer, giving her more time to settle down. I went back down two floors to the basement and proceeded to try to focus. This would become the single greatest battle of regret and unforgiveness I held towards myself. If I had walked into that bathroom then, could she have been saved? Was the Holy Spirit trying to speak to me to go into that bathroom?

Trying to work on ministry, I couldn't shake this sick-to-my-stomach feeling. I decided to go up and talk to her. I noticed that the bathroom door was still locked, and the water was still running. I went to the door and knocked. No answer. Knocked again, no answer. I said, "Hope, I just wanted to tell you I love you." In that moment, after there was still no answer, for the very first time, I feared the unthinkable had happened. I got into our hall closet as I began to shake from my inside out. I pulled a coat hanger we had in there that we used to poke through the hole of the doorknobs when they were accidentally locked. I forced my hand to be steady enough to unlock the bathroom door and tried to push back the thoughts of what I might see while telling myself, "She would *never* do that."

What happened after I opened that door is still blurry, traumatizing, and an out-of-body experience. I feel it is not healthy for me, my family, or anyone reading to know every detail, so as not to cause any more trauma. So, I am going to share a few thoughts and emotions of that moment but will not be sharing details of what I saw and experienced in that bathroom.

After opening the door and seeing the scene of death that was before me, my body, soul, and spirit went into protection mode. It felt as if I was being sucked out of my own body and into a realm where time stood still. It was like the horror movie I watched as a child that was burned into my mind and gave me nightmares, yet it was not a movie. I lost all ability to control my body. I wet myself. I ran to our laundry chute in the hallway and yelled as loud as I could for Faithanna. Somehow, in the shock, I was able to reason that she would hear me that way two floors down. Together, we got Hope in a position to do CPR. I stared with glassy eyes, ringing ears, and a nauseated stomach at Faithanna as she began to do what she was being trained to do as a nursing student. I knew I was close to passing out, as I had a history of doing so. I was shaken out of what seemed to be a dark hole I was falling into by Faithanna screaming at me to call 911.

My phone was still downstairs by my computer. I ran downstairs to the basement as fast as I could. I came up to the first floor and stopped to call. Not ever going back up to that bath-room and helping Faithanna with Hope will become one of my regrets I would have to battle. They say it is either flight or fight in a trauma situation. For me, I guess it was flight. I think I felt like if I did not have to look at her, what had happened, and her death would not become a reality. But I also believe, had I been in my right mind, I would have never left my eighteen-year-old daughter alone to deal with her sister by herself. It sounds so cruel to even think about it now.

As I tried to type 911, all I kept typing was Hope's name. Like I was texting her. Thinking about it later, I felt this scream on the inside of me, yelling her name as loud as I could. To wake her. To find her. To get her back. But the scream never could come out that day. My body was yelling in the only way it could do that day, typing her name over and over again on my phone. Finally, after about four tries, I got 911 typed out. The operator wanted me to tell her our address, and I think I had to try three times. I could not think, and I could barely breathe. My whole body was shaking uncontrollably by this point. She wanted me to stay on the phone with her until the ambulance arrived. I remember her telling me to meet the ambulance outside, and it was all I could do to focus on that one instruction. This was another reason I never went back upstairs. I heard Faithanna yell from the bathroom to me through the open front door, "Mom, when are they going to get here?!" I assured her they were on their way. It seemed like an eternity before the operator said to me, "They should be turning the corner on your street." I felt the ice-cold winter grass and mud hit the bottom of my bare feet as if to pull me back to earth again and make me face the reality of what was going on. I screamed down the street, "Hurry!" As they got out of the ambulance, I screamed, "She is upstairs! My daughter is doing CPR on her." I went to follow them upstairs, and they would not allow me to go up. I stood at the bottom of the stairs, and finding the only breath I had left in me, I shouted, "I command breath to come back into Hope's lungs now in Jesus's name!" I repeated it several times till I had nothing left in me. Faithanna came down the stairs, and we walked together to our first-floor office. Our walk was one of defeat, for we both knew Hope was already far gone from this earth. It was over before they ever got here.

I looked at the dust and mess that surrounded us that, just hours ago, I had big plans for. Our home was under construction. I was finally getting my new kitchen after sixteen years, and with it came new flooring through half of the first floor and a new office space. I slowly slid down the wall onto the wooden planks that were exposed. None of it mattered anymore. The idea that I had spent so much time picking out beautiful flooring, kitchen cabinets, and just the right sink seemed shameful to me now. As Faithanna sat down beside me, I did not embrace her or speak. I just stared. She asked me if I had called Samuel or Dad. I asked her to call her brother, and I said I would call Dad. The thoughts of how I was going to tell him rushed through my mind. How do you make that phone call and tell your husband that his Hope is gone? Jason suffered from severe anxiety that caused panic attacks, so the fear of losing two that day battered my mind as I picked up the phone to call him. I tried to see if I had the cell number of one of his friends at work, hoping to get ahold of them first so they could be there when I called. After realizing I had no one's numbers, I knew I could not delay. I needed to make the phone call.

Jason told me after, as I do not remember, that as he answered, I screamed into the phone, "Hopie has hung herself!" I do remember going up the stairs as I talked to him, and an officer was standing there, not allowing me to go all the way up. I asked them to tell me where I should tell my husband to go. I needed to know what hospital to which she was going to be taken. They said they were not sure yet, so I told him just to head home. As I hung up, I heard one of them say, "Maybe I've got something." We learned afterward from a friend that if there is no heartbeat or brain activity, the standard protocol is to call the time of death there, and the coroner comes to your home. We know from the report they never got a heartbeat back, and there was never any brain activity, so I believe that God had mercy on me and Faithanna that day. Perhaps the first responders heard my cry for mercy to God and took her to the hospital. I cannot imagine having to stay in that house and go through her whole death procedure there.

The next thing I remember is a female and male officer coming into the wide-open door of my house and asking to speak with me. As they were going over questions about what had happened throughout the day, I suddenly remembered that our ten-year-old daughter, Isabella, was about to come home on the school bus. She gets dropped off right at our driveway. "Oh my God," I said as I explained to the officers. They asked me what her bus number was, but I could not remember. I ran outside to our next-door neighbor's house and asked her to get Isabella off the bus for me and take her to her house. I said to just explain that Hope was sick and needed to go to the hospital, and we will pick her up later.

As I was running back into the house, our children's pastor's wife, Amy, arrived at our home. They lived close to us. I had no idea how they found out. I still don't. I know Faithanna was making phone calls to close friends, so somehow, the news traveled quickly to everyone. I do not even think I said anything to her. I just hugged her. Tears refused to fall, which seemed to make my pain worse. Soon after she arrived, they asked us to move to a different room so they could bring Hope down and get her in the ambulance.

What I did not know at the time was that as they were rolling her out to the ambulance, simultaneously, Isabella's bus arrived.

She saw her sister put in the ambulance. She was swept away to the neighbor's house, and we never saw her until we came back from the hospital to tell her the heart-wrenching news. Looking back, we should have taken her with us. I regret making that decision with our neighbor for many reasons now, but at the time, I did what I thought was best in chaos. I hate that she was without us after seeing such a traumatic image of her sister. But I know the Father was with her.

An officer approached Faithanna, Amy, and me and told us they were going to UC Hospital and that we should leave now and meet them there. At that very moment, Jason walks in the door, not able to breathe, in a full panic attack. He looked like he had just gone through hell to get home, and now we must head to the hospital. He told me he could not go right away; he needed a minute. He told us to go with Amy, and he would follow us. We went to the car and, in silence, started the ten-minute drive to the hospital. I remember Faithanna talking to her brother on the phone in the back seat, telling him we were on the way to the hospital. I told her to tell him to get a flight and come home. For the first time since the moment it happened, I felt like I had enough of my faculties to reach out to someone myself and ask for prayer. Of course, the first person that came to mind was my close friend Cindy, whom I had reached out to last night and in Lowe's just earlier in the day. I called her, with no answer, so I texted her the words, "URGENT." That is all I could get out.

I felt like we walked into that hospital in slow motion. Like we had all the time in the world. I think we both knew what we were about to walk into. The outcome seemed almost impossible to be anything but death. They put us in a private waiting room where many of our church pastors and friends were already waiting for us to arrive. I sat down and decided I needed to call my parents, who lived four hours away In Knoxville. I called my stepsister in California right then as well because I knew she would fly to Knoxville and drive them here. My parents (my mom and stepfather) were both battling cancer, and I did not want them trying to drive on their own in emotional shock. Soon after, a nurse asked for the parents of Hope. Jason was not there yet, but they insisted I go with them to Hope. Faithanna stayed behind in the room with all our friends. When I walked into that room and saw a machine pumping Hope's chest, I was certain I was going to pass out. I felt like I was looking at her from a million miles away. They told me to grab her hand and tell her I loved her, that she could hear me. I tried, but I felt so nauseated and heavy. My ears started ringing, so I knew if I did not sit down, I was going to pass out. I asked for a chair. In a monotone voice, I began to tell her I loved her. It did not even sound like my voice to myself. It was cold and non-emotional. I did not believe them. I did not believe she could hear me. She was not there. Her soul had already left her body, and she was in the arms of Jesus. Afterward, I thought about what they said and realized they probably do that so loved ones can receive closure. Our senior pastor's wife, Kimberly, came into the room and stood beside me. She had just gotten to the hospital and had found out I was in the room by myself. As she held my hand, they called her time of death. All I can remember saying to Kimberly at that moment was, "Wake me up from this dream." I wanted to be present. I wanted to say goodbye to my sweet Hope. I wanted to cry. I wanted to scream "NO!" but nothing would come. All I felt like doing was running as far away from that room as I could. I told Kimberly to please get me out of there.

I looked at everyone in the waiting room, and I fell into the arms of the first one I came to, which I think was my friend Dana, and yelled out, "My baby is gone! My baby is gone!" I asked her why I could not cry. "What was wrong with me?" I pleaded. She said I was in shock.

Then people started asking me where Jason was. He never made it to the hospital. I looked at our children's pastor, Chris, and he said he would go get him from our house. As I learned later, Jason could not physically drive himself, and the officers apparently are not allowed to drive people (ridiculous under these circumstances). He was too distraught to move. Chris got him and drove him as fast as he could to the hospital. When he arrived, he wanted to see her, but they told him protocol did not allow anyone now to see her until the coroner did. They also advised him to wait and not see her until the viewing because, at this point, her body would start showing signs of death, which would be traumatic to see. He insisted on seeing her.

Jason and I got interviewed by someone else who took a report on what happened that day. Holding a trash can in front of me, I wanted to throw up as I went through everything again, but it would not come out. I remember them asking me details of how I found her. Nobody should ever have to describe that about their own daughter. Jason was released to see her after about an hour. I regrettably did not go with him, but our senior pastor, Barry, did. Again, I'm not too sure why I did not go, I should have been with my husband, but I was not even in my own body, much less my own mind. I know I was afraid of looking upon Hope's lifeless body once again. I just did not know how much more I could take. He told me later that he did pray over her resurrection.

When all was done, they told us to go ahead and go home. There was nothing more we could do. I remember Jason, Faithanna, and I got into Chris's car in deafening silence. I do not remember which one of us broke the silence and said we needed to figure out what we were going to say to Isabella when we got home. Jason and I decided that, for that night, we would just tell her there was an accident in the bathroom and Hope was with Jesus. We just could not get the words suicide out of our mouths, especially to tell our ten-year-old daughter.

When we got back to the house, the three of us went and got Isabella from our neighbor's house and led her into the front room of our home. We told her what we had discussed, and the three of us held her while she cried. After that moment, I realized we were not alone in our home. Apparently, Jason had given someone a key, and our church family had come in while we were at the hospital and brought food and drinks. Walking into the living room we were greeted with love and open arms. I fell into the arms of my long-time friend, Carmen, who was like family to me. Our families had been knitted together over twenty years ago, and they were broken over the news.

I knew that I could not stay in that house that night. Our home had become the burial ground of our daughter. Sixteen years of memories, laughter, family pictures on the walls, hopes and dreams shattered on the floor of a bathroom I never wanted to step into again. I could not breathe in the house. With so many loving people around me, all I wanted to do is run away. Our sweet pastor arranged to put us, our son Samuel and his wife Jasmine (who were flying into town that evening) in a hotel room. We left as quickly as we could.

Chapter 2: Saying Goodbye

I remember finding the remote of the TV in the hotel and putting on the Food Network channel to try to drown out the nightmare in my mind. One of my close friends, Dana, offered to stay the night with us in the hotel. I thank God she was there because we did not want to be alone. She sat on the couch and held Faithanna as she cried all night. Instead of the numbness and shock Jason, Isabella, and I were feeling, Faithanna was feeling the reality of what had happened all night. Where I could not cry, she never stopped. Although I will be forever grateful Dana was there to hold my sweet Faithanna, I should have been the one doing it. I wanted to be the one doing it. I just seemed to be trapped, imprisoned, in a mind and body not my own.

Samuel and his wife, Jasmine, arrived that night. I was relieved to have our family all together. We needed Samuel, who was a bit removed from the trauma of it, to help us get through the next week. Remarkably, Isabella fell quickly to sleep that night. I am sure it was shock, God's protective mechanism He has placed in every single one of us when our body, soul, and spirit cannot take any more trauma. It manifests differently in everyone. Thank God it was sleep for her that night. Jason lay awake, crying and moaning off and on all night. If I slept at all, it was only moments of sheer exhaustion. It was the longest night of my entire life.

As the sun rose, we started getting texts and phone calls. Pastors from the church arrived with breakfast. I had not eaten since lunch with Hope and was still so sick to my stomach that I could not stand even to smell it.

I remember Isabella coming to me that morning and showing me the first supernatural sign that God knew and He was with us. Isabella had a Bible trivia game on her iPad. Each day it gave a theme. The theme of the day, the day after we lost Hope, was "HOPE!"

It was time to face saying goodbye to Hope. How do you prepare to bury your daughter, who was full of life and joy less than twenty-four hours ago? We did not even know where to start. Thank God for our church family and pastoral leadership, who literally stopped everything in their busy schedules to take our hands and walk with us through the most painful days we would probably ever have to endure in our lives. Not only did they walk us through the process, but our entire church family poured out extravagant love to us. So much that many outside the church saw what the love of Jesus looked like for the very first time. We were never left alone for the first two weeks. After that, friends stopped by daily to check up on us and to help us in so many ways. A meal was brought to us every day for the first entire month, and the congregation donated over $2,000 in gift cards that continued to help us for almost a year. A "GoFundMe" page was created that raised $10,000 for us to help with the funeral cost beyond our insurance and the inevitable decision we would make to sell our home and move.

I recently heard Rick Warren speak about losing his son to suicide and how life-saving it was to have friends who were willing to minister in the "ministry of presence." When something so life-altering and tragic happens, hope is found in the presence of those who are just willing to be silent and sit with you in the midst of the shrapnel. I pray if you find yourself in the middle of your life-altering tragedy, you also have friends who know how to minister in the ministry of presence. If not, pursue those who you trust and express to them what you need. Sometimes people just do not know what to do. They fear doing the wrong thing. Do not be afraid to ask. It may save your life. Rick Warren said he would not be ministering today had it not been for his friends. I can say from experience having friends willing to just be there in the silence with us was our lifeline of healing. Without them, we would have fallen so far into a dark deep ditch that I am afraid we would have never found our way out. Jesus calls us to be in a relationship with others, to bear each other's burdens. You cannot go it alone.

We stayed for two days in a hotel that our church provided for us. After a discussion with our pastor, the church parsonage was offered to us as a place to stay until we figured things out. Faithanna and I especially did not want to go back to the house. Reliving that trauma would be sheer torment. I was feeling a sense of fear I had never felt in my life. I would eventually learn that the fear I was experiencing was coming from the trauma of finding her. I knew we had to go back to the house and grab some items. Sadly, we would also have to pick out the clothes our daughter would be buried in.

I will never forget being told by the coroner's office that we needed to pick out a turtleneck for her if we planned on a viewing for her because of the markings. Oh my God, have mercy, the TV series I hated even seeing the advertisements for flashed into my mind. We were walking in some kind of freak reality of what I could not watch on TV, and it was my own daughter who had become a victim. Not a victim of any person, but of the devil himself. The evilest of all evils. I knew Hope did not have a turtleneck at home because she hated them. Dana took me to Kohl's to pick one out for her. I remember walking into the department store I had shopped at countless of other times with my girls. Hope was never a big shopper, but in recent years she had learned to enjoy it more. I am sure part of the motivation was shopping with Mom to get what she wanted for free, as teenagers know how to do so well. But I also felt like it had become a place the Father was giving us to share together. For the past two Black Fridays, our girls and I had made a marathon shopping spree of over thirteen hours straight. As I walked into Kohl's, zombified in my flesh, the moments of laughter and joy shopping with Hope ran through my soul like a serrated knife in an open wound. I watched as mothers and daughters shopped, as people went about their day, and it seemed so cruel that life had not come to a screeching halt for everyone else. I gazed with no expressions, wondering if I would ever be normal again. I picked out the first turtleneck I came to and held it in my arms like I was holding a baby. It would be the very last thing I would buy for my sweet Hope to wear… and she hated it. As I was buying it, I felt anger rise in me for the first time. Not at Hope, but rage at Satan, who made me buy such an article that Hope would never wear. Didn't she deserve to at least be buried in what she loved most to wear? I would later find out they did not need the turtleneck. Apparently, good makeup hid what we should not see (and what I had already seen). Perhaps this was the mercy of God for my sweet Hope.

The day now had come to go home, or what once was our home. Walking into the door of our home that had become a place of safety, comfort, family, laughter, and memories for sixteen years now felt like I was walking in the devil's den. He had stolen it all from us. His voice mocked me as I looked at the living room where I had countless of prayer gatherings with my closest friends.

Walking up the stairs, I relived the last time I had walked up those stairs to check on Hope and find her lifeless. I walked quickly past the bathroom that was shut and stayed shut until we moved. I would never go back in there again. Going into Hope's room, my legs shook, and my stomach was turned upside down. The half-full Starbucks coffee cup still was on her desk. Her scent was still in the air. Her pajamas lay on the floor. Her bed was still undone, inviting her back to lie down for another night.

But she would never come back to her sweet bed we bought her as an innocent young three-year-old with pigtails. The yellow sweatshirt I had bought for her for Christmas, after running to three different stores to find her size, was in a pile right where she had taken it off. She loved yellow. Her room was in a bright, beautiful yellow. I picked up that yellow sweatshirt and was crushed under the weight of the memory. I wanted her to know at Christmas how much I loved her and how special she was. I wanted her to realize that I would hunt deep and wide to find an overpriced sweatshirt just because she wanted it. Oh, how I did not know at the time that I would bury her in it. My heart could not take too much more. I tried to push back reality in order to do what I had to do at that moment. My fingers shook as I went through my own clothes, trying to pick out what I would need for an unknown amount of time, and of course, for my daughter's funeral. The nausea I had felt in the hospital the night before had never left me. My stomach turned as my entire body was reacting to what had happened.

As we went to walk out the door, another close friend was about to knock. When I saw her, I broke down for the very first time. Tears that refused to fall for twenty-four hours now fell like a waterfall that could not be stopped. What I did not realize at that moment was Jesus was beginning to heal me through the gift of tears. Satan had seemingly taken the entire lives of our family and crushed them under his feet for himself. But Jesus was coming in like a flood to crush Satan under His feet for us. I was broken, but I was still a child of God.

My friend Cindy flew in from Fort Worth within just a day of us settling in at the parsonage. My parents and stepsister drove in from Knoxville as well. The church and the church parsonage were located on a hundred-acre-old horse ranch. It was a farmhouse that had been added onto over the years, so there were plenty of bedrooms for everyone to stay in the house with us.

Cindy stayed in the large master bedroom with Isabella and us, and Faithanna had friends who stayed with her every single night in her room. The amount of warfare we went through each night was dark and haunting. I remember waking up in the middle of the night from a couple of hours of sleep after my body just could not take anymore to hear Cindy interceding for us. She fasted and prayed for us day and night for the first week. I cannot tell you how much we needed that and how much it brought love, comfort, and healing to our souls.

As we walked the cemetery with our pastors, Faithanna, and Samuel to decide where Hope's body would be put to rest, it all seemed unreal. How did we get here? What are we doing? As we chose her resting place, we realized it would be our place too. Although we knew that Hope now lived with our heavenly Father, we could not stand the thought that she would be laid to rest with no family around her. Jason and I decided that day to purchase the two plots beside her for ourselves. The uninvited and inevitable death of all of us became so real that day. That had to be hard for Samuel and Faithanna to hear us not only pick out their sister's burial site, but ours too.

I woke up with an indescribable emptiness each day that went by. The sun arose every morning on my horrifying reality that Hope was no longer on earth. I could not go to her room to wake her for school as I did each morning, fix her fruit smoothies for lunch, and tell her I love her and to have a good evening at work. All purpose for living seemed to be lost.

February 2, 2020, was the day of her memorial service. I woke up from just a couple of hours of sleep as the sun was rising. I went into the solarium that was built into the master bedroom of the old farmhouse. With windows surrounding me and acres of green grass underneath a crisp February frost, I sat down and simply stared. I had no words. I am certain Jesus came and sat beside me that day in the silence. I could not cry, I could not pray, I could not reason what I was about to do that day. I would celebrate my sweet seventeen-year daughter's life in the presence of her death-stench body. I stretched my eyes out as far as I could see as if searching for Hope to appear on the horizon. Perhaps I was longing for both my Hope and the Father's hope that day, but emptiness swallowed up the very breath I was struggling to breathe. I got up from where I was, and with all the grace of heaven at my disposal, prepared myself to see my daughter's face for the very last time.

We were in awe that day of how many people attended her funeral service. We greeted people for over two hours and finally had to stop to start the service. At least a third of the people we never were able to greet. We had over 1,500 in attendance. I remember standing up on the stage and looking out of the sea of people and saying to myself, "Hope, how could you have ever felt unloved on this earth? Look how loved you were." I felt both gratitude for the incredible amount of love shown, but so deeply saddened that she did not know it in her own heart, at least while on earth. It might have saved her life. What a tragic waste of love not to have received it while on this earth.

Samuel and I decided to speak at the memorial service. Friends have asked me how I had enough strength to do that. I was not in control that day. The Father began to speak to me about what to say in the quiet of the night before. Satan had his say, but the Father would have His, and He would get the last words. I became His voice that day. The grace on me was nothing I have ever experienced. Here is what I said as Jason stood beside me and held me up:

> Hope: The expected assurance of the Father's promises on earth.
>
> I was six weeks pregnant when I hemorrhaged. Think-ing we were losing our precious child, we rushed to the

hospital to find out I was pregnant with twins. We had lost one of them, but one of our babies was still healthy. Hope Noelle White, saved to be on the earth for such a time as this. Seventeen years of hope manifested. She is a word sent from heaven to earth. Her purpose will not fall to the ground but is eternal and everlasting and will continue to manifest and bear fruit through everyone who was touched by her life. God's Word will not return void. If you have been touched by her sweet and precious life, you now have a responsibility to carry on Hope.

Hope for the Father's peace. Hope for the Father's love. Hope for the Father's freedom. Hope for abundant life. Hope for healing. Hope for deliverance. Hope for joy. Hope for eternal life. Hope for hell to be made smaller and heaven to expand its borders.

Listen to my words, children and youth, Satan will pay for what he has done, and God will have His vengeance. Our justice will be found in your anointing, Faithanna, Isabella, Samuel, and to all of your generation. All of heaven has been given to you—what will you do with it? Run the race. Do not stop until you have destroyed the works of the enemy and set the captives free. Go with a fire for Jesus and allow the eyes of a hopeless and desperate world to watch you burn until nothing is left but the perfect and holy love of the Father. I rebuke the voice of Satan to speak into your life—your ears will be deafened to him. But receive the Word of the Lord; you are His child. God almighty, the Creator of everything you see, chose you to be His child and chose you to be born for this time. You are loved, wanted, and called. You have His DNA, and at the sound of your voice, you can bring heaven to earth. Do not fall asleep. Do not reject the gift and calling within you. Be the love of the Father and His Hope manifested to your generation. You are not just natural; you are supernatural. You have the resurrection power of Christ flowing through your veins. Go and do the impossible in the name of Jesus and for His glory.

Moms and dads: Your time is short. You have a short time to hold your children. To love them with the Father's love. To pick up the arrows God has given you, aim them at their purpose, and release them with God's power and presence. Let our story remind you of that every single day. Awaken from your slumber, for the Father has need of you. He has given you His Word. What will you do with them?

To our Hope: We love you with an everlasting love that has no boundaries on this earth. You are not gone from us, but just have stepped behind the veil into the holy place of the Father's presence. You loved us well. Your presence here with us will be missed beyond words, but until we see you again, we will take your laughter, your sense of humor, and your compassionate heart to give to others and manifest hope every single day.

Hopie, you are beautiful.

Chapter 3: The Wrestling

Unlike a child's death through sickness or even a car accident, suicide brought many unexpected things through which we had to navigate. There was a full investigation done by detectives. Hope's computer, iPad, and phone were all confiscated the day of the incident, and her closest friends—and ours—were all interviewed. A full autopsy investigation had to be done as well. They sent her phone away to try to break her password but were unable to do so. Thankfully, we were able to capture her pictures off iCloud. No one ever found anything to answer why she did what she did that day or even clues leading up to what happened. Jason took full responsibility for all things with the investigation, knowing I was not strong enough to handle it. Things seemed to drag on for months, which made the grief even harder. Four months after her passing, we finally got her death certificate. To our shock, it had details of her death that were extremely hard to read. Even many months later, I answered a phone call from the police department stating they had her clothes if we wanted them. We chose not to get them as no good would come of it, only more trauma.

Some big decisions had to be made after her funeral. It became evident that we were not going to be able to live in our home. We decided to sell it and purchase a new home. As I mentioned before, we had been in the middle of renovating. We had no kitchen and no flooring on half the first floor. Once again, due to the overwhelming kindness and love of our church family, several contractors in our congregation got together and finished our renovation at no cost so the house could be sold.

We were just trying to learn how to breathe again for those first three months after losing Hope. Finding a new home seemed like an impossible mountain to climb. But God met us right where we were and helped us find the perfect home. Selling our home of sixteen years, the only home our children remembered, and purchasing a new home was not easy in the middle of our grief. We found it difficult just to be able to think and process big decisions. For months we had "trauma brain." The brain shuts down partial functions to protect itself from the trauma it has endured. Simple tasks were hard, and memories were very short-term. But the day we moved into our new home, we received God's sweetest confirmation. One of the contractors that helped with our old house renovation was helping us move in that day. As soon as he stepped into the living area, he remembered previously being in our new house. It turns out that he and the other contractor friend who had worked on our old house had both done major renovations to our new home four years previously. Our steps were being ordered by the Lord. The first night in our new home was exactly three months from the date of her passing. We chose that day intentionally. Here is my Facebook post from that day:

> Our steppingstone. Our first night in our new home. This day is bittersweet, as it also marks exactly three months to the very day our Hope found her way to the loving arms of Jesus. We chose this day as a stepping stone in the Jordan River of our lives. We have been on the back side of the desert for three months. I cannot begin to describe to you the measure of pain and emptiness we have experienced. In moments, hours, and even days, our breath was taken right out of our lungs. BUT this day. The third month. We stand on our stepping stone and say to our enemy, "You did not win!" A strategy of defeat filled with hopelessness and regret was your game, but resurrection power was our gain! Hope is not dead, but alive, and we are not hopeless,

but will arise with fire on our tongues and power in our bellies to declare the goodness of the Father to a hopeless and needy generation. She is not forgotten nor absent from our lives. Her fingerprint is on our hearts, and we will find her in our lives as we move forward. Resurrection power and life marks this day, our stepping stone.

The day we got the keys to our new home.

The day of our home dedication.

So now let me widen your view and address the overarching timing that this all happened. It was the year 2020! The year of COVID-19 and the great shutdown of America and the world. We buried our Hope in February, and by March, schools and the marketplaces of the world were shutting down. There was panic everywhere for food, water, toilet paper, and cleaning supplies. God had provided for our every need as the parsonage was well stocked, and families were still bringing us food despite what was going on all around us. The Lord takes care of the broken-hearted.

I remember walking into a store to get a few items and nothing was left on the shelves. With everyone wearing masks, only their eyes, which seemed to have no hope, were exposed. It was bizarre that what we were experiencing personally seemed to parallel what the world was experiencing on a corporate level in many ways. Was this just a coincidence? I still don't have the answer, but I can't help but shake at the fact that even the way in which she died seemed to have a prophetic insinuation of what was happening to the world. Those who were suffering or dying from COVID had their very breath taken from them, just like my sweet daughter. Those who were left were saturated in fear and trauma. In many ways, the trauma came from the news media and constant reminders of death all around them. People were walking around sucking in the very mask that covered most of their faces, trying to catch their next breath themselves. It seemed the culture was suffering from a slow death of hope. Each day brought more suffocation, more lifelessness, more silence, more isolation, and more sterilization until hopelessness draped the nation.

By seemingly divine intervention, the isolation of COVID did not seem to affect us or the close friends who continued to stay by our side. Even though my parents had both just gone through bouts of cancer, with my dad recently finishing a round of chemotherapy and radiation, they continued to travel from Knoxville to be with us. Just as Jason was trying to go back to work, he was forced to start working from home. This created a perfect environment for us to walk through healing and restoration together. Even as I am writing this book over a year later, Jason is still working from home. The Father seemed to somehow be able to pull us out of the environment we were stuck in and make exceptions for us. We had a grace and covering that kept us, in many ways, untouched by what the entire world was going through, even down to getting the virus. Our three kids got the virus, and it lasted for several days for them, but nothing too serious. Despite not isolating from them or doing anything to sanitize the house, Jason and I never contracted it.

As the months flew by, I kept myself busy making our new house into our home. But eventually, there was nothing left to do. All the boxes had been unpacked except for Hope's. We decided to place all her things in one area of our basement and go through it together when our friend Cindy flew in from Texas later that summer. I knew this was going to be a very difficult thing to do since I had not helped pack up her things. Those boxes represented her life of barely seventeen years. It was wrapped up in fifteen boxes in the basement. Some days I would walk by and just try to smell her scent. I was scared to open any box. I knew it would be like a knife turning in my bleeding heart. But I so longed to see her clothes, smell her scent, touch what she had touched. It became a tug-of-war in my soul.

As all the busyness of the first three to four months after her passing wore off, it was time to face the reality of life without Hope. Each one of us found ways to cope and distract ourselves from the emptiness and sorrow. There was no "getting over it." You do not lose a child from suicide, grieve for a few months, and go on. This was when the hard work of healing and restoration began. The percentage of marriages that stay healthy after the loss of a child is low, and it did not take me long to realize why. Trying to find "family" again was extremely painful. Every time we were all together, it just reminded us of what was and was not anymore. We had to learn how to talk to each other, how to laugh, and how to love again. We all went to counseling for a time, and some of us still do. We are all grieving and healing in different ways. Miraculously, I can attest that my marriage to Jason is stronger now than it ever had been.

PTSD (post-traumatic stress disorder) is a real thing, and there was no doubt we were all experiencing it to some degree. Having been the ones to find Hope, Faithanna and I have had the most issues with PTSD. Someone would cough, choke on something, throw their hair a certain way, or say a certain comment, and I was standing in that bathroom, experiencing it all again. It was extremely hard to even take a shower or be alone in a bathroom for months afterward. I panicked when I heard a bathroom door close or lock. We told Isabella we never wanted her to lock a bathroom door again. I just could not re-live that over and over again.

While we were still at the parsonage, Isabella went to take our dog (really Hope's dog) out to the bathroom. It was dark and rainy, and we were living on a farm with lots of acreage and a pond. After a few minutes, she had not returned. I went out and yelled for her with no answer. Immediately, I was standing at that bathroom door again, saying Hope's name with no answer—only this time, it was Isabella. I went into this out-of-body experience again and ran all over the yard, yelling her name. My heart was racing, tears were rolling down, and all I could think was that I was losing another child. I even went back into the house and yelled for Faithanna like I did the day of the incident. I'm sure I was pulling her back into our trauma as well. We both went back out and Isabella came walking around the corner. She was on the other side of the house, and it blocked the sound of us yelling for her. She had no idea why I was so distressed. I just felt out of my mind. It took hours to come back to my senses and stop shaking.

The days and nights became a battle of sheer willpower to get through. Going to bed at night brought too much silence that opened the door for my mind to run wild in the memories of the trauma. Before Hope's passing, many in our family would go to sleep with worship music playing all night long. But now I noticed I was responding to worship music with a deep sadness. The first three months, I avoided listening to it altogether. This was unusual for me because I was known as a worshipper in my family. I played worship music all day long in the house and spent hours praying. I had even written books on worship. Now, suddenly I could not lift my voice to sing to the Lord, pray, or even listen to a worship song. A "wrestling" had begun in my soul, and I was trying to run from it in fear. I had unrealized anger towards God, who I lovingly called Father. I would eventually have to come face to face with it. The mornings were just as bad as the nights. I would wake up with a deep emptiness, reminding me that yesterday's reality was still today's. I would go through the shock of not having Hope all over again. This went on for close to a year.

After the distraction of finding and moving into a home was over, I felt lost. I did not know how to start really living again. Jason was working from home, trying to find his new "normal" of work life, and Isabella was starting to go back to school. Faithanna was going to college and working. My day should have been spent working on family ministry for our nonprofit, Chosen Stones, and spending time with Hope—who should have been doing her senior year at home. Nothing seemed as it should be anymore. I had no desire to do ministry again—ever. The night we came back to the house from the hospital, I wanted to find every book I had written and burn it. How could I speak to families and think I had anything worthwhile to say to them? My daughter died in my house while I was writing in the basement, two floors down.

The thought of ministry made me want to throw up. I felt like such a hypocrite. The house felt empty, and I had no purpose.

My mind raced daily with the images of the death I had witnessed and the shock that my family of six was now a family of five. The life I once had was left shattered on the floor of a bathroom I would never step foot into again. A line in the sand had marked two separate lives. I felt stuck in between two worlds. One that felt like another lifetime ago was filled with such joy, promise, laughter, and... Hope. Along with the distant memories lived the "if's," "should haves," and "would haves." My past had become a painful place now as I looked through broken glass that threatened to distort situations, words, and circumstances. The lenses through which I now looked led me to question everything. The other world—my present and future—was the world of the unknown. A place seemingly without Hope. It was a world that I did not want. But I also knew if I stayed in the middle, I would surely die. I was afraid of forgetting the world of my past but did not know how to embrace the world that stood in front of me.

On top of this incredible grief and loss, Satan was preying on our vulnerability as a family. Often when the suicide of a loved one happens, it destroys relationships that are left behind. The battle of reconciling and healing the pain, guilt, and regrets, if not addressed in a healthy way to the Father and through counseling, can manifest in accusations, assumptions, and deflections that cause division between loved ones. This, unfortunately, happened to our extended family members. Satan used their brokenness, and ours, to throw stones at all of our bleeding souls. I have learned this is not unusual. If you find yourself in similar situations, remember we do not wrestle with flesh and blood but against our adversary, Satan. He has no mercy on the brokenhearted. Hurt people *hurt* people. I am certain we all did that to each other in many ways. Accusations and rejection hit me like salt in an open wound. The pain was almost unbearable at times, and I was at my lowest through the strife in our family. Sometimes it just takes time for everyone to process their own grief and get to a healthier place for reconciliation to happen. For others who perhaps do not rest in the Father's help and love, reconciliation may not happen completely, but forgiveness is a requirement in order for you to heal and find hope and peace again. Through deep soul searching and the discovery of my daughter's own private struggle with low self-esteem and self-hate, I have found a new compassion for those with similar suffering. If someone has hurt you during your time of great suffering, it most likely is not about you; it is about their own eternal struggle. You need to give mercy, grace, and love. The place of greatest suffering is the place of great vulnerability. Satan will use anything to keep you down.

The cold jagged cliffs of suffering, regret, and self-hatred brought at the hands of the accuser that tormented Hope now threatened to overcome me too. My lifeless, breathless shell of flesh labeled "Mom" now struggled between wanting to live and find my breath again and surrendering to the hopelessness that consumed every part of my being. I was not and have never been suicidal in my thoughts, but I was in a place I had never been. I knew I had two adult children and a ten-year-old daughter who still needed me to be a mom and a husband who needed me to be present as a wife. I still believed in Jesus, but I just did not know who Jesus was to me anymore.

I was wrestling with the Lord after seeing the carnage of the life I thought we had in Jesus that was now shattered on the ground in a million pieces. The torment of the guilt, shame, failure, and questions robbed me of peace. The image replaying in my mind daily was a horror movie that took my breath away. It assaulted every good, beautiful, and treasured memory of a life lived weeks before. Along with questioning my self-worth as a mom and family minister, who had given her whole married life to raising our four kids in the ways of the Lord and teaching them how to have an intimate relationship with the Father, I questioned the very foundation of my belief in Jesus. What I thought I knew about Jesus was abruptly and painfully ripped out from underneath my feet. What remained were questions. I questioned the Father's protection, Word, sovereignty, and love in the ruins of our past.

The "wrestling" in the aftermath of a great tragedy usually does not end with close family, especially in the case of a teenage suicide. For the first year after Hope's death, we would hear from parents and youth who had their own place of "wrestling." The ripple effects of her death brought emotional and spiritual turmoil to so many who had grown to know and love her. Jason and I felt even more guilt knowing that our daughter's death brought trauma and so much grief to other teenagers. The lives of families were disrupted for months as the youth tried to process and cope with the idea of Hope taking her own life. COVID did not help as the youth were isolated away from their friends and the joyous occasions of teenage life. Graduations were canceled, prom canceled, youth trips canceled, and youth ministry altogether was canceled for almost six months. The timing was terribly hard for her friends and their families to receive counsel, understanding, and healing.

The first year of any person's loss of a loved one brings all of the "Firsts." My first birthday, my first Mother's Day, Jason's first Father's Day and birthday, and her siblings' first birthdays without Hope. Then there was our first Christmas without her. Christmas was a difficult one. I started decorating really early to try to fill the home with the spirit of Christmas, but the absence of the *one* was always there. We found a few things to do to honor her that first year. We wrapped a dog toy under the tree labeled "from Hope." Revie was Hope's dog, and she always gave him a Christmas gift. We left her stocking up on the mantel. On Christmas morning, the *one* stocking left hanging was a grim reminder of the laughter of Hope that did not fill the room. We tried to gather around the table, and all spoke of a good memory of her, but for some, it was just too painful to do. It was important that we recognize her as still part of the family and that we address the "elephant in the room," but it was incredibly painful at the same time. We did eventually find some joy that day, and we knew the Father's presence was with us. The next "first" would be her eighteenth birthday, three days after Christmas, on December 28. Hope loved to paint and so we decided to have a painting party and invite all her close friends and ours. It was a beautiful night of honoring Hope and healing. This "first" forced us to move forward. It was God's natural and sovereign way of nudging us to continue to live.

In the months of this great wrestling, I was reminded of a vision I had over fifteen years ago. I was in my home worshipping the Lord. I was taken into a deep place of soaking in His presence. I saw myself on an altar tied down. I was wrestling with the ties trying to free myself from their grips. I was uncomfortable and wanted to escape. After a time, I realized that I was not going to get free and abandoned my idea of escape. I gave in to the altar that lay beneath me. In that place of surrender, I found great peace, love, and hope. I arose from that place and entered the Kingdom of Heaven. My eyes were open to see into the spiritual realm and the mysteries of God.

Could this be where I was? Was the Father taking me through a time of great wrestling to ask me to abandon this one thing at the altar? Was this the key to finding peace? Was this the key to my healing and finding the mysteries of the Kingdom that had been revealed to me?

Could this be where you are at today? Are you wrestling with God? Are you in a season of suffering? Is the Father asking you to abandon the altar? Are you desperate for peace and hope? Come follow me to the invitation for all of us who find ourselves in that same place.

Chapter 4: The Invitation

As the wrestling intensified, I tried to find my footing again. I began to hear the Father speak to me:

> "Alicia, I am inviting you into a new place of trust. The trust I am inviting you to will shift your entire perspective of my truth and my kingdom. This higher place of trust will demand everything to be consumed at the altar. There will be nothing left in your hands. Are you willing? It's the place of abandonment. Your place of resurrection and hope."

I saw myself high on top of the Grand Canyon, just like the picture of Hope that I used for this book. I remember so well when that picture was taken. I had taken the kids to surprise my parents in Arizona. The Grand Canyon, being only a bit over an hour away from where they lived, was one of the first places we wanted to go. I was a nervous wreck the entire time, however, because I am terrified of heights. All the kids practically ran to the edge of the cliff, where there were no railings to hold them back. I stood from a distance in awe of the view that stood before me. The kids kept beckoning me to come closer.

The Father had placed me back on that cliff of the Grand Canyon in a vision. I saw Hope at the edge, but I was too fearful to go near. I was vulnerable and exposed to the harshness of the rough terrain, fearful of the edge of the cliffs that threatened to send me tumbling to my death. My whole body shook as I tried to find a way out of the jagged edges of the stones that had put me on this mountain of suffering, loss, and wrestling. I kept my distance from the edge but was drawn to the beauty that lay beyond. The beauty I knew was there but could not seem to find. My fears of the unknown and what might happen if I got too close kept me from walking forward.

I heard the Father's voice beckoning me to come closer to the cliffs. My breath seemed to be stolen in the clear cold air of the mountain. My view was frightening but unhindered. Each cliff I could see now had become a roadway. "Didn't I tell you I would make the mountains a roadway?" As I walked closer to the edge, I began to see with the Father's eyes and perspective. His heart spoke: "Abandon to my ways and my thoughts. Who are you, great mountain?"

I recognized those words from a scripture the Father had given many years ago:

> "So, he answered and said to me:
> 'This is the word of the Lord to Zerubbabel [Alicia]:
> 'Not by might nor by power, but by My Spirit,'
> Says the Lord of hosts.
> 'Who *are* you, O great mountain?
> Before Zerubbabel [Alicia] *you shall become* a plain!
> And he [Alicia] shall bring forth the capstone
> With shouts of "Grace, grace to it!"'"
>
> Zechariah 4:6–7 (NKJV)

I saw five cliffs that represented a place of great suffering and wrestling within my very soul, and there was an altar at each one. Each had a place of worship. They were places of sacrifice but, deeper yet, places of abandonment. The cliffs were transformed into a roadway as I left everything at the altar. The roadway was one of peace, purpose, life, and a beautiful promise lying ahead of me. It was a place of resurrection, life, and hope. The great mountain of cliffs that threatened to take my life became the place that gave me life.

I could hear the Father say, "You will find hope at the edge of the cliff. Come close, my daughter; my love will keep you safe. It's time to let go." The Father was inviting me on a journey of abandonment.

In today's Christian culture, abandonment is not a term we hear much. It seems to carry with it negative inferences and images that we become uncomfortable with very quickly. Surrender is the term that is written about, sung about, and taught about in Christian circles. At first glance, they sound synonymous with each other. Though they do have similarities, they are much different from each other.

I think of surrender as the first step on the road to Emmaus. Personally, surrender becomes the tender first step we walk with the Father as he beckons us to the cross. In this place of surrender, we find an exchange of the heaviness of life for the light yoke of Jesus. We find the love of the Father stretched out on a cross meant for us. Jesus had taken our place. As parents, the image of surrender fits inside the story of Abraham and Isaac. Abraham, in an authentic desire to obey and please the Father, takes his child by the hand and goes up to the mountain of sacrifice. Did he do it knowing in his spirit that the Father really would not take his son? We do not know. But we do know he went through the motions of being a good father and parent but surrendering his son into God's hands. But his surrender and obedience came with a ram in the thicket. God had provided a "way out" of the imminent death of his child. Abraham's reward was to hold his promise (his son) in his arms for the rest of his days on earth.

Surrender, with the awareness and even expectation of the ram in the thicket (Jesus on the cross for us), is what we like to do most as children of God. We shout out with sounds of joy as we pat ourselves on the back and say, "I surrender all," thinking we have made our hike up the mountain of sacrifice. But what happens when that ram never reveals himself... when the cross is made for you and not Jesus? What happens when you take your child by the hand and lead them to the foot of the cross, but find out you do not get to hold your promise for the rest of your days? What happens when you look in horror at an altar that is marked with your child's death, and the reality that there is no way out begins to take hold? You "abandon."

You see, surrender is to reluctantly give up what you take ownership in. What you feel is yours, with a list of terms and conditions to go along with it. When an army surrenders to another, they do it by force or a feeling of "having to." There is no real trust in the one they surrendered to. Surrender is not necessarily giving up your rights to the person to whom you surrendered. Just because a nation must surrender land to another nation, it does not mean they do not feel that land is still theirs. A feeling of rights, or ownership, often creates a battle of trying to take back what you think is yours. We often do the same thing with our surrender to the Lord. We lay something down, and with a lack of trust and full abandonment in the Lord, we try to pick it back up the next day.

I knew the invitation was not to surrender but to fully abandon.

Perhaps your altar is not for your son or daughter, but for you or a loved one you have lost tragically. Perhaps it's for a marriage that ended in a tragic loss. Perhaps, like me, you expected a ram in the thicket, and it did not come. Healing didn't come, deliverance didn't come, reconciliation didn't come, and seemingly Jesus didn't come. There is only one thing left to do… abandon.

Abandonment. This is the longer, wider, higher, and deeper walk on the road to Emmaus, the Grand Canyon, the road less traveled. Abandonment is the relinquishment of the right and ownership to what I hold most dear in my heart. Abandonment is to hold no desire or feeling of ownership of a thing or person and willingly give up all rights and responsibilities to someone else. One who is fully abandoned to the Father has no desire for ownership of their own life or even the things they love. They have complete trust in the One who will take the best care of your treasure. Abandoned children of God do not have the desire to take back what was never theirs, to begin with. They live in peace, not engaging in the struggle between their spirit and flesh. There is no power struggle between deity and man in this place of holy abandonment.

Abandonment requires the release of all "buts." We all have "buts" that are hidden behind the best costumes at the masquerade ball right before our eyes. They are the best-kept secrets of unrelinquished control and expectations over our life. They hide in the depths of our souls, keeping our flesh in a place of comfort and security.

If we dare to unmask them in a place of honesty and vulnerability, they sound a bit like this: "Take my life, Jesus, *but* not my job. Do what you want, Jesus, *but* do not make me do that. I give you my marriage, Jesus, *but* I am not the one that needs to change. I give you all of me, *but* don't let me get sick and die." If parents are honest, the biggest *but* in the room for us is, "Jesus, I give you my children, *but* keep them safe and far from harm's way." But when the Father takes away your *but*, and what you believe contradicts truth, what foundation will you stand on?

In one moment, what I thought I knew about Jesus and the Father was pulled out from underneath me, and the mask suddenly came off to reveal my "but" that had been there all along. After all the years we spent declaring the Word over our children, pleading the blood, interceding, teaching them the Word, taking them places to encounter His presence, the worst of all darkness had just happened. How could He allow this to happen? I trusted Him. But did I? The harsh truth is that I trusted Him on my own terms. The "buts" stood between us.

In Luke 24, a story unfolds after the crucifixion of Jesus. The stone had been rolled away, and the disciples were told He had risen, yet they could not believe it. Two of the disciples were on the road to Emmaus. They were clearly in shock and wrestling to find answers. They were trying to reason with each other, unable to see the truth and the answer right in front of them. They thought they had surrendered to following Jesus, but suddenly, their own expectations of what that should look like fell short of the reality they faced. Jesus had died and left them alone. What He said had seemingly not come true. Where were the promises? Where was the victory? The religious people killed Jesus, and He had let them. Where was the ram in the thicket? Hopeless, they walked on this road, wrestling with who Jesus really was and what their own future would look like. Fear had set in, despair and disappointment. Joy and a feeling anything was possible gave way to pain, suffering, and defeat.

Even when Jesus, being resurrected, joined them along their journey to Emmaus, they could not perceive truth. His words hit their soul, but trauma and suffering clouded their ability to receive them. They were stuck.

I can relate to the disciples, can you? They could not move past the pain and suffering. All they could see was death, not resurrection life standing right in front of them. When reality hits the deepest parts of our soul and screams, "This wasn't supposed to happen," suddenly, we begin to question everything. Truth becomes relevant to our circumstances. We see through the lenses of trauma and not through the lenses of the kingdom. Nothing makes sense anymore.

It wasn't until they invited Jesus to abide with them in their place of suffering that their eyes were open to see life and hope in the eyes of Jesus himself (Luke 24:28–32). Jesus took the bread, broke it, and gave it to them. Then, there, at that moment, their eyes were open. When they communed with the crucified Jesus, when their pain came face to face with His, they were able to see and abandon in truth. In that moment of abiding with the one who has all the answers, finding the answers did not matter. As they ate of the word made flesh, their brokenness became the roadway that led them to hope again. The suffering of Christ brought them to the resurrection of Christ. Eating the bread broken for them, that is Jesus, filled their empty souls that were just moments ago hollowed out from hopelessness, disappointment, and unmet expectations. The "buts" disappeared when they ate of the *one* who was broken for them. The bread became the answer and the only *one* that mattered. A beautiful picture of abandonment.

However, the greatest example is Jesus Himself. In His own place of suffering, Jesus had a moment of wrestling. "Abba, Father, all things are possible for You. Take this cup away from Me; nevertheless, not what I will, but what You will" (Mark 14:36, NKJV).

Like Jesus, in the agonizing pain of my grief, I also have asked God, "Why did you permit this cup of suffering?"

Jesus felt the weight of the cup the Father permitted for him, and even but for a moment, felt so overwhelmed by the pain and suffering that He asked for the cup to be removed from him. Jesus wrestled in His pain. This has always moved me deeply. He addressed the Father in His power and deity and declared His ability to stop what was happening. Yet quickly, Jesus came to the resolve that if it was the will of the Father to drink from the cup of suffering, he would abandon to it. Jesus, knowing that the cup of suffering would birth redemption for mankind, drank from its bitterness and pain. The scripture tells us the sweat that dripped from his flesh in the garden was droplets of blood. As he drank from the cup of agony, his body dripped off the very substance that would bring redemption to mankind. Jesus's cup of suffering brought resurrection life to us all.

There was a passage of scripture that the disciples began to ask about this cup. They wanted, in love and ignorance as to what it really meant, to drink of the cup with Christ. Jesus responded, "You do not know what you ask. Are you able to drink the cup that I am about to drink, and be baptized with the baptism that I am baptized with?" They said to Him, "We are able." So He said to them, "You will indeed drink My cup, and be baptized with the baptism that I am baptized with..." (Matthew 20:22–23, NKJV). They did not understand fully what that meant. Jesus was essentially saying to them, "You will suffer for me." They would partake of His death and crucifixion, but because He drank first and paid the penalty of death in their place when they drank from the cup of suffering, resurrection would be the fruit of it.

"That I may know Him and the power of His resurrection, and the fellowship of His sufferings, being conformed to His death" (Philippians 3:10, NKJV). As the disciples, we have an opportunity to know Christ in His suffering, to drink of the cup with Him, and reap the rewards of His resurrection. The requirement of such a shared cup will only come through abonnement. Other than Jesus, I know no other example better than the first church disciples after His death and resurrection. They suffered much and abandoned it all. They surely did drink from the cup of suffering.

I knew the Father was extending an invitation to me to come to the edge of the cliffs and abandon all that I wrestled with. My hands would be left empty, burned at the altar of abandonment. Yet, I also knew it would require me to extend an invitation back to Jesus, inviting Him into my place of brokenness, vulnerable and with nothing between us. I knew as I laid aside my fear and walked towards the invitation of the Father to abandon, I must also invite Him into the place of my pain and share a drink from His cup of suffering. I had to embrace the pain, just like Jesus.

When I stopped fighting Jesus about the cup of suffering in my hand and instead embraced it, knowing all the fighting in the world wasn't going to change it, my suffering took a shift.

When I came to the end of myself in the valley of the shadow of death, I encountered Jesus in a way only those who die can, in the fellowship of his suffering. My lifeless body, soul, and spirit encountered the suffering Lamb of God, and a sovereign union happened. We supped from the same cup. I experienced a sacred place within Christ I could never have known had it not been for my journey of pain. As I invited Jesus to drink from the cup of suffering with me, and I with Him, I began to sweat. My suffering of death and pain was beginning to produce a manifestation of life. Dripping from my brow, redemption and the goodness of the Lord began to fall.

It was not easy, it was not painless, and it was not quick, but it was the only hope I had of getting out of the very dark cave of such tragic loss and grief.

Perhaps you are reading this book and find yourself in the shadows of death. Your own place of suffering. Suffering comes in all different sizes and shapes. The Father does not measure it little or small. He is a compassionate, loving Father that takes no pleasure in seeing His children suffer at all. But he does take good pleasure in drinking from the cup with us. His cup of suffering always leads to life, hope, and redemption.

"Be still and know that I *am* God" (Psalms 46:10, NKJV). It is often a scripture we use in our times of great suffering and wrestling. The word "still" in this scripture comes from the Hebrew word "Rapha," which means to be weak, let go, to release. To be still is to abandon and know that He is God.

No matter what your place of suffering and great wrestling is today, I speak courage inside your very spirit to let go, to abandon, and to sup with Jesus. If you allow them to, the next chapters will lead you on a journey to the edge of the cliffs. It will be a place of death, loss, hopelessness, and fear. It will be a place of wrestling with who the Father truly is and who you are in Him. It will be a place of courage to embrace the cup the Father has permitted for you, and to drink of it with Him. Yet, it will be a place of transformation, where the Father's love and ways invite you beyond the veil of suffering and into the holy place of abandonment. Each jagged cliff beckons you to come closer to the edge, finding a deep place of trust you may not have known yet in the Father. You will stand, kneel, or lay at the edge of the cliffs until the place becomes an altar of worship. Through abandonment and suffering with Christ, you will become a roadway of resurrection and hope. Perhaps your place of suffering is not like mine. Ask the Holy Spirit to reveal what your personal cliffs are as you read each chapter. You may not wrestle exactly with the same things I have fought, but I believe you will find your own story in this story of hope. And the God of hope will radiate power and strength to heal and restore you.

Chapter 5: The Cliff of Loss and Grief

Jason, Samuel, and Cindy had packed up Hope's room within the first week of her passing with Samuel and some close friends. Since I could not stand the thought of walking back into that house and seeing her things in her room like she was just at work and coming home, I asked him if he would do this. It was so incredibly painful. I will be forever grateful for my courageous husband, who stepped up and did what I could not do.

We had many sweet friends to help us throughout the process of packing up our home and preparing to move. It was during COVID, and the whole world was in quarantine. But our closest friends never left our sides and were willing to be with us no matter what. At the time, COVID was the least of our worries, so we paid no attention to it.

We were about to move, and I needed to help Jason dismantle some furniture and do some last-minute things in preparation. The house felt so empty of life and breath. We got to Hope's room and my heart was crushed under the weight of the shell of a room that remained. We had to dismantle her bed. As we got on our knees to unscrew the frame, I flashed back to the excitement and joy we had felt buying her "big girl" bed when she was a toddler. It was a white, farmhouse-style bed, and Faithanna had one just like it. The girls were only fifteen months apart and shared a room until Faithanna was a sophomore. There was a ledge that went around the bed for the mattress to sit in. As our hands touched the ledge, we both felt and saw the same thing... Hope's hair. She had long, thick, dark, beautiful hair. We collected her hair in our hands like it was precious gold. Tears flowed uncontrollably. I instantly remembered that within the last week of her life, I had bought her vitamins for her hair because she thought she was losing too much. We held the last evidence of our child's life in our hands. For a moment, I could feel her. I imagined holding her chest close to mine as I held the hair near my heart. The loss and grief were shattering our hearts into unrecognizable pieces.

It seemed so cruel and unjust that the Father was asking me to endure a loss so unthinkable and unimaginable. The cup seemed too heavy to hold. After all, He did not have to endure such loss… so I thought. Jesus, the son of God, had died, but He got His son back in three days. I was expected to live the rest of my days on earth without my Hope. I thought my loss was greater than His. How could He ask this of any parent? Months later, a precious friend of mine who had lost her son tragically many years prior would give me heaven's perspective. The Father says that a day is like a thousand years (2 Peter 3:8). Could it be that the Father felt three thousand years between the loss of His son and being reunited with Him again?

In my deep loss and grief, I found myself wrestling with letting her go to God and wanting her here on earth with me. One day I would trust God with her, then the next day, I would tell Him to bring her back to me, and the loss was just too much. In a moment when I was struggling the most, the Father gently said to me, "What is it that you have always taught your parents in ministry? Is Hope not mine? Did I not give her to you for a season to partner with me and raise her? Why are you demanding ownership of what is not yours?" These words hit me like a ton of bricks. I knew she was the Lord's. I knew I had to abandon my right to Hope. For months after that, when I would begin to feel a great loss, I would say out loud to the Father, "I abandon my right to Hope. She is not mine and is now home."

I was led to listen one day to a minister, Corey Russell, who was speaking about the "gift of tears." Corey had lost his son and knew my grief very well. It was the story in the eleventh chapter of John where Jesus raised Lazarus from the dead. For months after Hope's passing, I could not bear to hear or read about that story. I remember a guest speaker coming to church soon after her passing, and Jason and I almost walked out when he started relaying this story. How could I rejoice over Lazarus being raised from the dead, yet the Father chose not to do the same for our Hope? But the more I tried to avoid this story, the more I found it everywhere. On this particular day listening to his message, I knew there was something in this story for me.

Jesus was four days late, by His choosing, to see His friend Lazarus. Yet when He got there, He wept. What did He expect to see? He had been dead for four days. If Jesus was that upset, why didn't He come earlier? Scripture goes on to tell us that the resurrection of Lazarus was basically one big object lesson to demonstrate the power of Christ and the glory of the Father. But my heart questioned Jesus's tears. Why did Jesus really cry? He knew He was about to raise Lazarus from the dead. He knew he was coming back to life again. He could not have really been grieving the loss Of his friend, could He?

I believe at that moment, Jesus was inside the heart of you and me. He looked pain and torment right in the eye that day. He looked across the sea of humanity, spanning for decades and centuries, and felt the grief, sorrow, torment, suffering, and anguish of what each one of us would have to endure on this earth by the darkness of death and loss. He looked death in the eye, not as one who would die, but as one who suffered with the living. He knew we would be living in a world full of sin, the curse of us all unto death. We would be living in a world with evil, darkness, and Satan, the prince of the air, who would come to each of us to steal, kill, and destroy. He wept for the suffering that life would bring each one of us.

In the early moments, when the shock would wear off and I could feel the depth of the pain, I had something supernatural happen to me. I heard Jesus weeping with me. As I would invite Him into my pain, and we would drink from the cup of suffering together, Jesus wept with me. If you are under the weight of suffering today, whatever it is, Jesus longs to weep with you. Take the time to invite Jesus into your place of suffering and listen for the sound of His cry. There is healing found in the torn soaked rob of Jesus. His tears will mix with yours and fill the cup you're drinking from with His perfect love.

> "You keep track of all my sorrows.
> You have collected all my tears in your bottle.
> You have recorded each one in your book."
>
> Psalm 56:8 (NLT)

Along with weeping with Jesus, I also found myself breathing with Jesus as I drank from His cup of suffering.

In the early days of my grief and suffering, I found myself taking deep breaths through my nose and exhaling through my mouth. The deep, violent blow of what had happened would suddenly hit my stomach, and my insides would shake. There were no words, not even tears sometimes. There were only breaths that seemed to form from deep within my spirit. The unintentional reaction of breathing in deeply despite the utter feeling of death was unknowingly renewing life within me. The Father was in the garden of suffering with me creating new life out of my dead soul. I was breathing in all of heaven and exhaling the pain that earth had handed me.

"And the Lord God formed man of the dust of the ground and breathed into his nostrils the breath of life; and man became a living being" (Genesis 2:7, NKJV). Mankind was just a lifeless, hopeless shell until the Father breathed life into our nostrils. The moment God's breath hit Adam's internal being, the blood of our

Father ran through his body, carrying life to every organ, bone, and muscle. The moment the Father breathed His holy, perfect, loving breath into man, a union was created between His blood and ours. He joined our spirits together for eternity. We became one and were made whole. The cup of suffering brought a breath from heaven to heal me.

As you invite Jesus into your place of suffering, allow the ruach, the breath of God, to permanent every part of your being. Imagine with every deep breath that Jesus is filling you with all of heaven, and with every exhale, the ugly and painful blows of suffering are blown away. Let's practice that now.

Isabella, only being ten-year-old when her sister passed, found her own way of dealing with grief and loss. She wrote a song about Hope that a friend put to music for us. This is her song:

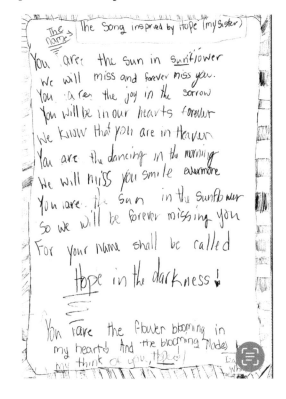

The name → The Song inspired by Hope (my sister)

You are the sun in sunflower
We will miss and forever miss you.
You are the joy in the sorrow
You will be in our hearts forever
We know that you are in Heaven
You are the dancing in the morning
We will miss your smile evermore
You are the sun in the sunflower
So we will be forever missing you
For your name shall be called
Hope in the darkness!

You are the flower blooming in
my heart. And the blooming blade
my think of you, Hope!

Over the last year, COVID has created a demand for worship songs about the hope of God. As we personally fell into a season of hopelessness, so did the world. The culture had a stench of death. Great worship leaders began to make a unified sound of Hope to fill the air through the spirit of the Lord. It was uncanny how every song on the radio echoed the word "hope." In a season where it was almost impossible for me to pick up the Bible and read, the ministering sounds of His Word filled my soul with songs of hope.

One of the songs that brought incredible healing to me was "You Keep Hope Alive" by Mandisa. I thank God daily that Jesus died on the cross and rose again, so my Hope could live!

In Hope's 2020 journal, written just weeks before she took her life, she had a list of predictions that she would have accomplished in ten years.

It included:

- Graduated from college
- Living alone
- Have a tattoo
- Have two dogs
- Not live in Ohio
- Own a Jeep

Also included in this journal entry was a beautiful piece of artwork displaying the places she desired to travel. Her travel bucket list as it was titled.

It included:

- Utah
- Nevada
- Alaska
- New Zealand
- Bora Bora
- Colorado

- South Dakota
- Virginia
- Oregon
- Montana

One of the great places of loss and grief for our beautiful seventeen-year-old was that she was *only* seventeen. She had her whole life ahead of her. I felt robbed of every parent's joy of seeing their child grow into adulthood. My heart never gets to see her walk out of her destiny and call the Father's purpose for her on earth before she was conceived. The joy her life would bring to others was cut short. The life experiences that the Father planned for her vanished. She would no doubt experience tough and hard things, but there would be things full of His perfect love and joy. Her high school graduation, going to Colorado as she had planned for her graduation vacation, meeting the man the Father had willed to be her helpmate, her wedding, and having children would not happen. All these things I grieved for her and for the rest of us. "Hope" deferred makes the heart sick.

Yet all the dreams and hopes she and I had for her life on this earth paled in comparison to what she is experiencing now. Marriage and having children are tremendous joys on earth, but they are for the earth. She has become a virgin bride and her groom is Jesus. No man on this earth could ever be better than that. I would have loved to have taken her to Colorado but imagine what vistas she now beholds. She sees colors unimaginable, life unspeakable, and rivers clear as crystal.

Hope, who loves to write, who loves to draw and paint, who loves her dog, Revie, and her turtles, Skirt and Sheldon, will be forever beautiful. Her deep laugh is contagious, and her sense of humor is medicine for the soul. I describe our Hope in the present tense because I know who God created her to be. It did not begin here on earth, and it will not stop here either. She is alive and very much our Hope. But now she is walking in the highest potential of who God called her to be in heaven. Hope is now the best version of who God created her to be. She did not begin on earth, and she did not end here either.

I want to stop right here and address a controversial and sometimes very cruel ideology that people claim with suicide deaths, especially within church culture. There are some who believe that if a person who claims to be a Christian dies by suicide, they go to hell. Taking your own life is a sin, and that sin has eternal consequences. I do not subscribe to this thought. Why? Because sin doesn't send us to hell. It is sinning without a savior that sends us to hell. If sin sent Christians to hell, heaven would only be for God and Jesus. No one is perfect and without sin but the Father and His Son. We are eternally saved and promised heaven solely because of Jesus and what He did for us on the cross. Our salvation is not best upon perfection. It's based upon our belief in the man, the savior, the son of the living God, Jesus. A Christian who sins, through repentance, has the power, grace, and love of the blood and body of Jesus to cover their sins.

I do agree that suicide is a sin. It goes against the very love of the Father who created us in His image. However, suicide deaths are no different than dying from addictions of all kinds. The person struggling is mentally and spiritually weak and sick, and at that moment, unable to fight the demonic battle against them. Their heart wants to stop taking the drug, and they want to live and not die, but their soul is gripped in a demonic battle that many lose on earth. But Satan cannot touch their spirit, which has already been committed to the Father. Jesus gives them the victory of heaven. The Father is merciful and full of unmeasurable love. Do you think that a child of God, who has loved and served Him, would be sent to hell because they simply didn't have the strength mentally or spiritually in a moment to defeat Satan's attack? I don't serve that kind of God!

What about those who took their life and never received Jesus as their savior on earth? When those who have attempted suicide have been interviewed, one of the first things they say is they regretted it as soon as they attempted. They are not in their right mind. In fact, most have a false sense of "doing everyone a favor" by dying. A lie, no doubt, from Satan Himself. I believe there may be a moment between heaven and hell. A moment full of mercy, love, and space to receive the Father. Do I know this for sure? No. But none of us do. Who can judge a man's heart but God? And who can judge the Father's love for His children by God Himself? Suicidal thoughts are sheer torment, and God sees the heart of man long before He sees their sin.

A friend gifted us a farmhouse wall chalkboard when we moved into our new home. Isabella wanted it in her room, and soon after, she wrote this scripture on it: "What has been will be again, what has been done will be done again; there is nothing new under the sun" (Ecclesiastes 1:9, NIV). When I saw what she had written, my jaw dropped. She had no idea this was my favorite scripture of the Bible. It is an obscure scripture that not many would probably call their "favorite." For a child to choose to write this down is even more strange. The Father was speaking to me through Isabella's prophetic act.

After all these years, I never fully understood why the Father highlighted this scripture to me until now. My heart has never more longed to hold on to the promise that everything that once was shall be again. I will be reunited with my Hope. But more than that, the beautiful place of intimacy and holy perfection between the Father and His children in the garden shall be again too. Hope is home, face-to-face with the One who knew her before she was conceived. Hope is walking and talking with God in the cool of the day, in His beautiful garden.

I had a very real encounter with this truth several weeks after we buried Hope. I had not gone very many places, but I needed to go to the bank and get a few groceries. One of my precious friends, Diane, offered to take me. She unknowingly took me to the very grocery store and bank that I was last at with Hope. At that time, she did not know, like most people, the story of that day. I said nothing but decided to press in and face the inevitable. I went to the bank and the teller recognized me right away. I was stunned she knew what had happened, and she came over and expressed her condolences. It was hard to keep it all together. As we walked out of the store, Diane asked if I wanted a hot chocolate from Starbucks. Again, she had no idea that I had walked in those footsteps with Hope to get her coffee that day. I hesitated but said "yes," and asked her to go to the one across the street, outside of the grocery store.

Before I tell you what happened next, I want to tell you a short story of Christmas Eve 2019. Hope was working at her Kroger that day. It was a "bogo" sale at Starbucks, so Faithanna asked me to go with her. We decided to go to the Starbucks inside Hope's Kroger so we could say hello to her. I bought Faithanna a coffee, and I got a hot chocolate for free. We went over to the bakery and said "hi" to Hope. We told her we would see her soon at home. That day when she got home, I felt very sad that I had taken the hot chocolate for myself instead of getting Hope something. After all, she was the one working on Christmas Eve. I told her I was sorry. She said to me, "It's okay, Momma. I know you don't get your hot chocolate very often."

Fast forward to Diane offering me a hot chocolate while doing my errands. We went through the drive-thru and to the window to pay. When we got to the window, the employee said, "No need to pay. The car ahead of you paid for you." I started crying, of course, right away and could hear Hope's voice say to me again, "It's okay, Momma. I know you don't get your hot chocolate very often." You could call the gift a coincidence, but

I believe the veil between where she was living and where I was living was very thin that day.

Many years prior to Hope's passing, I had shoulder surgery. Because I had an emergency tracheotomy when I was a child, there is scar tissue built up in and around my trachea that can cause issues when intubating me for surgeries. The hospital decided to try a nerve block to avoid having to fully intubate me for this surgery. After coming home, I began to have a reaction to the nerve block sight. Jason called the helpline given to us, and they instructed him to take the bandages off and rub down the area. When he did this, my heart and breathing stopped, and he said I went into convulsions. The nerve they used was the one that controls your heartbeat and breathing. Apparently, it was inflamed. After about a minute, I was awakened by the sound of him screaming my name.

This was the encounter I had during that short time. I have never shared this publicly. I am someone who can become skeptical of all the near-death experiences that others have had. It isn't that I do not believe they exist. I just don't know how much the tales are embellished. This is my unembellished experience.

I was in a place full of bright, radiating white light. I felt nothing of this world, only sheer peace, joy, and comfort. I had a conversation with someone. I cannot tell you who, as I saw no face. I do not remember what the conversation was about, and I was abruptly pulled from this place by the sound of Jason's voice.

I sensed over time that the conversation was spirit-to-spirit and hidden from my soul, which may be why I do not remember it. I have asked the Father many times why I had that encounter. I am not sure that the Father knew I would need it for this exact point in time, but it has brought me incredible comfort to have experienced what my daughter may have had immediately after her death. I was living, but just in another dimension, and now so is she, forever.

I had Jason put this on my phone screen, and it is still there to this day:

She is living, I am living, just in two different places.

"While we look not at the things which are seen, but at the things which are not seen: for the things which are seen are temporal; but the things which are not seen are eternal" (2 Corinthians 4:18, KJV).

As I had the courage to step closer to the edge of my suffering and grief, I drank from the cup of suffering. I began to see with the Father's eyes. I had a vision of Hope in a time of worship. She was calling us to get up from where we were and "catch" up to the kingdom's pace, plans, and purposes. In our personal walk with our loss, so often we have felt that in order to move forward, we would have to leave behind our memories of Hope and what once was in the past. Yet I saw in the spirit something quite the opposite. I saw a vision of our Hope motioning for us to catch up. Life never ended for her. She just slipped into another dimension. But our earthly perspective kept her back in the past. My eyes were awakened to see she was not just still living, but she was ahead of us. Hope was in front of us, not behind us. She was embracing the fullness of the goodness of God and walking in the joy and glory of the Lord. She was walking with an eternal perspective. The reality of the kingdom revealed that we were not to walk and live in Hope deferred, but Hope immersed. Hope is all around us and is urging us to catch up to her.

This is for us all. Godly hope is the expectancy of the goodness of God, and it had gone before us and beckoned us to catch up. It is time to get up from where we are and brush off the dust of yesterday. We need not grieve what once was because that which shall be again is already in eternity. If we stay in the past, looking back to what was, we will never catch up to what is to be. Embrace the forward. Hope is found there.

Here I was. I had the courage to walk up to the edge of my cliff of loss and grief and abandon it all down at the altar before my Father, and the mountain before me became a roadway to resurrection, life, and hope.

I abandoned my thought that the Father asked of me what He did not experience Himself. I abandoned my right to Hope. She was not mine and was home. I abandoned my loss and grief for unfulfilled expectations on this earth. I abandoned my feelings of a cold Father who wanted me to be strong and stand in my faith, simply moving forward. I abandoned my thought that feelings do not matter to Jesus.

I worshipped at the altar of loss and grief with the Father, who understood my loss completely. I worshipped at the altar of loss and grief with my Father, who willingly gave His Son and suffered great loss and grief so that my sweet Hope could be who she was created to be and live eternally forever. I worshipped at the altar of loss and grief with the one who wept with me.

CHAPTER 6: THE CLIFF OF REGRET

When your child dies from suicide, there is an enormous amount of guilt and regret that is left behind in the ruins. When you have the privilege of partnering with God to raise a child, there is a full sense of responsibility to keep that child safe, healthy, and to live a life with joy. In my circumstance, I was a children/family minister who taught parents and children how to live a victorious life in an intimate relationship with Jesus. Where do I begin to tell you what fertile ground my mind was for Satan to walk all over it? I have also heard from many who have lost children and spouses through tragic accidents and even disease that there is a degree of regret as well. It is part of human nature to feel a since of responsibility for the one you love so greatly. Sometimes circumstances surrounding the death of a loved one can take you down a road of "maybe ifs," "should haves," "would haves," and "I didn't do enough" feelings.

Our entire family has battled on the hopeless ground of regret. It is a cruel, unforgiving place that steals all peace for what is impossible to change. Each one of our stories here are different, but I have been careful not to speak for anyone in my family but me.

My thoughts of regret began with the thought that I was the one who got in a fight with Hope on the day of her passing. It seems reasonable to assume that our argument put her over the edge that day. Honestly, though, I knew as a parent that I did the right thing by contacting her supervisor at Kroger. I knew the last words I had said to her, "I did it out of love," were true. I was never mad at her that day. My only concern was to keep her safe. I have never regretted what I said, but it has been what

I did not say that fills me with remorse. Hope was sitting in one of the middle cabin seats of our van, and Faithanna was up front with me. After I realized our conversation was going nowhere, I decided to be quiet. I do not recall ever using my mirror again to look back at her. Maybe if I could have looked into her eyes or seen her heart with the eyes of my spirit, I would have known the tormenting thoughts she was hearing. Maybe if I had paused long enough to look behind the wall she had put up to hide her own fear and insecurities, I could have assured her better of my love for her and how proud I was of her. Maybe if I had followed her up to her room and tried to talk to her more instead of staying quiet and going to the basement, she would not have felt as if no one cared. All of these "maybes" and countless more that have haunted my mind will never be assurances that I could have changed anything about that day.

Most would not have imagined Hope ever battling in her mind with self-hate and low self-esteem. She hid it behind many walls of protection. As her family, we knew of her struggle with self-esteem, but we had no idea just how badly she internalized her battle. She even went to counseling for a time, and the counselor never saw any warning signs. Hope was very engaged in our church youth group. She was loved by so many and had more friends than she realized. She was not what you would expect from a "suicidal" teenager. She was not depressed or shut up alone in her room all the time. She had a genuine relationship with Jesus. Our relationship was actually very good since she had started homeschooling because we had more time to hang out together. She worked almost forty hours a week and had good grades on her schoolwork. In fact, if she had her English credit, she could have graduated from high school in her junior year. She seemed to love life, and her joy and contagious laugh were evident to everyone she was around.

What happened that day to cause such a dramatic shift in Hope's outlook? I cannot tell you what went through her mind that day or any other day. She may have thought of suicide but did not act upon it. I never knew her struggle. We have never found any answers to that question or any others. I can tell you what I do know. Satan preyed on her low self-esteem. He used everything he could to attack her weakness as he does in all of us. Because of her own insecurities, Hope often felt offended, hurt, and rejected, and it often came out as anger. This was one of her many walls of protection. As a parent, the wall of anger made it difficult to navigate conversations and give life instructions to her. We found ourselves giving attention to the outward anger more than trying to find the true reason why Hope was acting the way she did. At some point, Hope began to believe the lies Satan was throwing her way. She began to believe that everyone thought about her the same way she thought of herself. This brought turmoil and tension in many of her friendships and family relationships, which fueled rejection and loneliness.

Hope was a writer, so she had many journals. We did not have the privilege of reading them until after she passed. When we were at the point of enough emotional strength to read the pages of what she had written, it was clear that Satan had isolated her and made her feel very lonely and unloved, despite being out-going and engaged with friendships and her youth group. Most of her journals were full of God's hope and encounters, but in a few, she dared to be vulnerable enough to pen her struggle with loneliness, even as young as twelve years old. As a mother, this broke my heart into a million pieces all over again. To think that she was surrounded by a family that loved her and even friends who did, yet she felt alone. Satan lies to us all. The mind is the true battlefield of any Christian. It is not the lie that defeated her. It was her inability to cast it down and not allow it to take root. Once it took root, it created a stronghold, shifting her reality and hijacking her decisions and her perspective on life. She kept this torment of her mind to herself, away from the help of anyone.

There was one moment when the Father gave me the ability to feel her broken heart. I was dropping Isabella off at school. As I pulled out to go home, I began to think about all the "should haves," "would haves," and "maybes," and the voices of others who had been used by Satan to accuse and judge me in my most vulnerable state. The level of condemnation and self-hatred I was feeling on that morning was deep, dark, and demonic. I was not and have never been suicidal, but the thoughts were darker than I had ever experienced. I pulled over on the side of the road as I heard the Father say, "To a degree, I have allowed you to feel what Hope felt in her darkest moments." I believe He allowed me to experience this for two reasons. One, so that it would shake me free from the slippery slope of hopelessness I was going down. Two, so that in the future, when I had the opportunity to allow our testimony, Hope's testimony, to minister to others, my level of compassion and understanding would even be greater.

I knew as I heard the Father's voice that I needed to make a change in my own heart and mind. I had allowed the accuser of my soul to fill me with countless regrets. I found it impossible to forgive myself. I was her mom. If it was anyone's fault, it had to be mine. Satan swung at me fiercely, judging the amount of time I really spent with her. Did I ignore her conversation with me when I was busy? Why couldn't I remember some of the things she told me? How much did I spend individual time with her? Did I tell her I loved her enough? Were there signs I ignored? Then Satan threw the low blows, questioning my responsibility to cover her spiritually. Did I intercede for her enough? Did I plead the blood of Jesus over her? Did I teach her how to cast down arguments in her mind? Did I open a door for the demonic in her life?

Beth Guckenberger, in her book *Relentless Hope*, describes it best: "I've seen (myself) swallowed by memories, guilt, shame, pain, the tricks the enemy uses to metaphorically grab (my) hair and push (me) under the water again and again and again. Then there is a pinhole of light (I) can see from my sinking position and it calls to (me). It is Hope. A moment in that light and the hope fills (me) with fight. It is time to reclaim and restore what the enemy was snuffing out. Look up, look out; believe it is yours for the taking. It is not what has happened, but what you are capable of. It is relentless; it is hope. It is yours. Take it."

I was falling into the same hopelessness of my daughter's lost battle. I had to find a way to face my past and forgive myself, casting down every vain imagination that comes against the knowledge of Christ within me (2 Corinthians 10:5). I had to find the courage to walk up to the edge of the "cliff of regret" and build an altar.

Not all regrets are bad for our souls. "For godly sorrow produces repentance leading to salvation, not to be regretted; but the sorrow of the world produces death" (2 Corinthians 7:10, NKJV). There is an appropriate place for Godly sorrow (Godly regret or genuine apology) that brings forth Godly fruit of growth. This was where I needed to drink from the cup of suffering with Jesus and use the regrets to make me better. We are all to learn from situations of life. This is one of the ways we grow in the Lord.

It is sometimes incredibly painful to look back on situations and circumstances and wish you would have done things differently, especially when the consequences of your actions cut so deep. I will never be able to "make it right" with Hope, no matter how much I change or repent. But drinking from the Lord's cup is full of mercy and love. Godly sorrow (regret) leads you to transformation into the image of Jesus. The best and only thing we can do with regrets of the past is to humble ourselves and learn from them. Sometimes the best you can do is realize that choosing to go low might take you down in the dirt, making mud pies with your tears, but you belong to an upside-down kingdom where the

Father desires to turn all things for your good. The mud is only providing rich soil for God's seed to bring forth fruit.

I have learned to be a better mom, wife, and daughter of God and to love above everything else. Our Hope was under so much torment in her mind that the pain came out as anger. What I thought was just rebellion or disrespect was agonizing pain that she did not know how to stop in her mind and heart. As parents, we were constantly responding to the anger. We demonstrated our love for her, but our reality was that life with her became hard and full of constant fights. The most agonizing pain I now feel is the inability to ever tell her I love her again. I want to wrap my arms around her, laugh with her, and hear her sing. My deepest regret is not affirming her enough. If she walked into this room today, nothing else would matter but telling her I loved her and holding her in my arms.

It is easy, as parents and even spouses, to get caught up in how someone is acting instead of who they were called to be. Frustration, anger, and hurt are weapons of the enemy. But if we err, let us err on the side of love. Affirm your children or your spouse in who they are in the Lord more than pointing out their shortcomings. Make your affirmations be what they remember most about your relationship with them.

My family will have the benefit of a better "me" because of what I have learned at the edge of this cliff called regret. I still struggle sometimes with the voice of the accuser, but I am learning to cast his voice down and forgive myself. I find it harder to forgive myself and put the past behind me than to forgive others. I have no doubt that Hope is in heaven and sees me only through the eyes of the goodness of the Father. She is not holding unforgiveness, pain, or regret towards me, others, or herself. I believe she is not just experiencing perfect love, but she has become perfect love. I also know the same about the Father. He holds nothing against me. He is not angry at me or disappointed in me. He sees me through the blood of His son Jesus. I can get through this. I can come out the other side and find that regret has just become a roadway to resurrection and hope.

But I also knew that Satan was going to try to give me a constant dose of worldly regret that would produce death in my life. This was much of the battle that Hope herself had.

The biggest ungodly regret that I had to cast down in my mind was not going into the bathroom the first time I went upstairs that day. I felt the cool breeze come across the basement, so I went up to get a sweater. I saw the bathroom door was still closed, and I knew she had been in there for quite some time. I stood there thinking I should go knock on the door and tell her that I loved her. I felt a stirring in my gut, but I shrugged it off because I never liked arguing with my kids. If I had gone into that bathroom then, instead of maybe twenty or thirty minutes later, could I have saved her? Was that the Holy Spirit speaking to me? I have taught families for years how to listen for His voice, and I had chosen not to listen?! The consequence of walking back down those steps and not going into the bathroom was the death of my daughter. In my own personal life, I know of two families who had this situation happen, but they opened the door just in time to catch their loved one in the act of attempting suicide, and the loved one lived. They "saved" them by going into the room. Could that have been what was going on that day, and I just refused to obey the voice of God? The adversary's voice screamed out, "You fool! You didn't even listen to your God like you teach others to do! You caused her to die! You could have saved her, but you didn't love her enough!"

Until the voice of the Father whispered into my ear, "I never called you to be her savior that day or any day. That is my job and mine alone. If I wanted to have saved her for earth, I did not need you to do it. I am a big enough God to have saved her. But I choose to receive her into heaven instead."

Saving her was not my responsibility. It is not our responsibility to save another person's life. We are not their savior. God may use us in circumstances to partner with Him, but if someone lives or dies, it is never within our power to decide. That is God's, and God's alone. We can't be God, and the moment we place that burden on ourselves or others is the moment Satan will defeat us.

This was profoundly freeing for me, but the battle has been real. I have had to battle with a culture that is propagating the exact opposite of God's words of truth to me in this pandemic. When COVID hit and mask and social distancing were mandated, there were advertisements, store intercom messages, signs, and social platforms, both of the world and of the church, that spread the ideology of: "If you truly love another, you must abide by these social distancing rules. If you do not, you will be responsible for someone's death." Isabella's sixth-grade school year after her sister's death was retraumatizing for her. The mask mandates at school went far beyond just using an extra precaution for the safety of everyone. There was no thought to those who suffer from PTSD or mental distress and anxiety and what masks do to them. The indoctrination of children to an ungodly yoke of being responsible for the life, death, and health of everyone around them was nauseating. Satan's voice echoed in a culture, "Don't be the one to kill grandma!" Isabella, suffering from both asthma and PTSD triggers, tried to keep her mask below her nose. She was bullied and told that she didn't care about others. Do you know what that does to a little girl who just lost her sister by suicide? It is cruel. There is a cultural ideology raising children and young adults to believe that they are responsible for the lives of everyone around them. It is a foolish lie from hell itself to try to get an entire culture and world to walk and live with self-god and condemnation principles that go against the very sovereignty and power of God, and God alone, to heal, save, deliver, and be the Lord over all life.

I do not want to seem insensitive to those who have suffered great loss through the COVID epidemic. You may yourself be one who has suffered great loss. I have lost an uncle, one of my closest friends lost her dad, and countless others within our church have suffered great loss at the hand of this virus. But the truth is, either God is God over COVID, or He is not God at all. You and I, or anyone else, cannot be any more responsible for keeping people from getting sick with COVID than keeping people sick from cancer, a cold, the flu, or any other sickness.

If you perhaps are one who has suffered great loss at the hand of the COVID epidemic, I want you to know there aren't enough "could haves," "should haves," vaccinations, and isolations to have saved your loved one. The Father alone was and is big enough to have saved them, but He chose to receive them in heaven instead. Sickness, both mental and physical, is part of a sin-filled world, and we will never be able to do enough to prevent it. Let go of any regret or what-ifs; the Father's ways are not our ways.

Another very strong ungodly regret I had was the feeling that while I was teaching families to put the spiritual needs of their kids first, had I done that with my own child?

We were invited to go listen to the McBeaths, our close friends and missionaries to Nicaragua, that stayed with us constantly for the first three months after. They were speaking at a church where I was previously the children's pastor. Jason and I played a major role in this church plant, and this church held a lot of memories for us. As I was sitting there listening to them speak, suddenly, all the memories came flooding through my mind of Hope as a toddler and preschooler there. All the times, I would pray in the back room with a group of intercessory ladies and Hope would play in the nursery. We did this once a week for two years, then moved the prayer group to my house. I was constantly dragging Hope to church events. I feel so grateful for those days, but I wondered if I neglected Hope's needs. Did I neglect my first calling? Was I so busy pouring into everyone else's kids that Hope just got the crumbs? The tears just rolled down as I remembered that little girl with pigtails running down the hallway. Oh, if I could do it all over again. She was always so good and never complained or made demands of me, so it made it easier for me to think I could do this and that. But was that good for her?

The Father spoke truth into this regret from Satan. He reminded me that I was not just raising Hope. I had Samuel and Faithanna at the time too. They are both now thriving, healthy, Jesus-loving young adults. Isabella, our youngest, is healthy mentally and is a very strong lover of Jesus. How could I allow Satan to place blame when the good fruit is so evident in my other kids? It was in Hope too. Our kids had the privilege of experiencing incredible spiritual things as children. They learned to encounter the Father in ways many children do not get to in our nominal religious settings. Hope's many journals are full of encounters she had with Jesus, prayers, and drawings focused on her personal faith walk. Her independent personal relationship with Jesus was evident. If I did nothing else well, I led her to Jesus.

There is no such thing as a perfect parent. The only one who is perfect is our heavenly Father. We do what we know to do, and He does the rest. His grace is sufficient for us, but it does not make us perfect.

I had an incredible gift from heaven as I began to unpack our new home and organize everything. I had kept many memory boxes of the kids' years of school. As I opened a box to determine how to label it, I found it to be one of Hope's memory boxes. Right on top of the box was one of Hope's school papers that seemed to be purposefully placed there by Jesus Himself.

I did "family gatherings" for five years, where I taught and modeled unique and spirit-filled ways for families to worship together. They were the most incredible years spent with our own kids before the Father. Yet Satan was making me question everything I had ever experienced with our kids. Were these family gatherings all for nothing? Did they mean anything to our kids?

But here, in this moment of pain, torment, and question, was Hope's own voice and eight-year-old handwriting telling me it did matter! I did make a difference! Within a little booklet created for Mother's Day was a list of reasons why she loved her mom. Number seven on the list: "Mom, you are beautiful because you are doing the family gatherings." Right there, on top of everything else in that box of school keepsakes, was loved expressed by my daughter and the voice of the Father reminding me that there is nothing more beautiful than when I poured out Jesus onto my family. Hope, even at a young age, saw beauty in how I was serving Jesus and my family.

I have learned to combat the constant voice of the accuser. I must do two things: put every ungodly regret in the fire at the altar and remind myself of Godly truth through beautiful memories that Satan cannot steal.

There is a page from a cherished book I received from a friend right after Hope's passing that has brought me so much peace at the cliffs of regret. It reads:

> "You could not have prevented this if you tried harder, prayed harder, or were a 'better' person."
>
> *You Are the Mother of All Mothers*, Angela Miller

I want to share some of my fondest memories of Hope at our family gatherings. I was using her to be "Jesus" in an object lesson.

Jesus

Here I was. I had the courage to walk up to the edge of my cliff of regret and abandon it at the altar before my Father, and the mountain before me became a roadway to resurrection, life, and Hope.

I abandoned my thoughts that I should have or could have saved Hope. I abandoned my thoughts that I was not a good mother to her. I abandoned my thoughts that I did not give her what she needed spiritually.

I worshipped at the altar of regret with the only one who could have saved Hope that day. God is her savior, not me. I worshipped at the altar of regret with my Father, who reminds me that there is godly fruit demonstrated and manifested in each one of my children, including Hope. I worshipped at the altar of my regret, learning that the one thing that matters most is love. The Father is making me into a better mother, wife, and woman of God through my place of suffering.

CHAPTER 7: THE CLIFF OF TRAUMA

One of my greatest regrets of the day Hope passed was my soul's response to turn away and run away from the scene of death. However, I need to address it here, at the edge of the cliff of my trauma, because my response that day was a result of the nightmare I was encountering. As parents, when our children hurt, we do too. We take on their pain and suffering in many ways. Why? Because our children are a part of us. Those who came from our very seed represent the hope of our legacy. They are bone of our bone, flesh of our flesh. When I looked upon Hope, covered in death and darkness in our home and in the hospital, I felt that same death and darkness. My soul wanted to do anything to escape it. I could not breathe. I could not reconcile that my heart that was still beating while part of me lay breathless in front of my eyes. For months, I felt as if I could feel her pain, torment, loneliness, and rejection. My mind began to fill in the blanks of her last moments on this earth as if I were experiencing it with her. It was almost too much to bear at times. The cup of suffering seemed cruel and tormenting.

My body, soul, and spirit had experienced a deep, tragic, life-altering trauma that caused post-traumatic stress disorder, or PTSD. To some degree, everyone in our family has experienced this. I do not understand all the science behind this disorder, but I do know when trauma is so deep, it creates a neurological pathway in your brain that, when triggered by one of the five senses, makes you feel like you are re-living that trauma over again. It was so incredibly painful and tormenting to live trapped in this trauma that I asked the Father in desperation to help me.

My prayer then, and still now, has always been, "Father, erase or replace my memory of that awful day." In many ways, the Father has honored my prayer.

One of the ways He has started to heal my trauma was to reveal to me the parallel trauma that the Father experienced Himself. There is something comforting to realize that my heavenly Father shared some of the same responses that I did in trauma. He shared the same experiences willingly because of His love for us all. My place of trauma has given me a deep appreciation and gratitude for what the Father and Jesus did for us. Have you ever wondered why the Father responded in such a way that made Jesus ask why God had forsaken Him while on the cross? Could it be that the Father Himself was dying right in front of His eyes? Could it be God Himself was drinking from the cup of suffering?

I shared a small measure of the pain that He must have felt watching His son die on the cross. Jesus took upon the death of all of humanity that day, and His own Father could not bear to look upon such darkness and suffering. Yet, He willingly allowed death to swallow His son for me, you, and our sweet Hope. As great as the darkness, pain, and suffering of death are, it still is not greater than the love of the Father. Because of the death of Jesus, Hope lives full of joy and life today. Jesus did not just die *for* us. He died *as* us. Bone of our bone, flesh of our flesh.

What I began to discern after Hope's death was that the trauma brought fear unlike any I had ever experienced. Walking through the scariest, most traumatic, and most tragic day of my life left me with a fear of death. I found myself fighting death more than I embraced the redemption and victory of life. I began to overreact to things, have irrational thoughts, and allow my imagination to run wild with worst-case scenarios.

What the Holy Spirit began to speak to me in my place on the cliff of trauma was if I continued to fear death, I could never embrace the truth of eternal life. Without that foundational truth, I would be tossed around by everything the enemy could throw at me. The fear of death would hold me captive and keep me from living with joy and peace. What I thought I believed in (eternal life, heaven, and God's sovereignty in my life) were ideas I had been taught and believed until I was forced to face death in the eyes of my daughter.

What I then saw, prophetically again, was a parallel struggle going on corporately in the church today in light of COVID. The time has come to evaluate what we truly believe about the Father numbering our days on this earth and His sovereign role in life and death. Jesus has already fought against death and won the victory for us. How much are we distracted by battling against something Jesus desires us to embrace? After all, is that not what the end of the book says: "And they overcame him by the blood of the Lamb and by the word of their testimony, and they loved not their lives unto the death"? (Revelation 12:11, NKJV).

I am not saying we are all called to be martyrs, nor should we wish upon ourselves or others to die before the time chosen by the Father… but doesn't He still choose? While we are in the midst of saving our life and each other's lives through measures that keep us from going, doing, and living the way God created us to be in relationship and fellowship, we should ask ourselves this question: "What are we scared of? What do we really believe about death and the Father's role in it?" After all, death is the only door to the promise of eternal life.

Although Hope took her own life, which is never the will of the Father, if I was going to get through the trauma of her death, I had to start seeing death through the Father's perspective. My view from the cliff must become heavenly.

We came to the celebration of Hope's birthday on December 28, 2020. It was going to be her eighteenth, so it had an extra weight of sadness on it. She would have become an adult that day. We decided to celebrate her birthday, without the guest of honor, by hosting a painting party. We invited friends and Hope's closest friends and painted canvases while listening to Michael Bublé… Hope's favorite singer. It was a time of healing for all of us. There is something therapeutic about painting. I felt so close to Hope that night. I understood why she loved to paint so much. Many of the kids went home and sent me photos of their pictures hanging in their bedrooms. Hope will be remembered.

As those who loved her began to wish her a happy birthday on social media, I began to think, *Father, how are you celebrating Hope's birthday?* I'm going to share what I heard: *We will be celebrating on January 29.*

That hit in my heart with a gut-wrenching thud and challenged me to seek the kingdom perspective. On a day that meant death, darkness, and total sorrow and brokenness, the Father was going to celebrate Hope's birthday? His ways are not our ways. I had been praying for months: "Father, either replace or erase the trauma and images that replay like a horror movie in my head." In His mercy and love, He was doing this the only way He could: through the mind of Christ and the kingdom perspective. This is the mercy found as we drink from the Lord's cup.

He was not denying or refusing to acknowledge the pain and tragic event of January 29, 2020. He could not change what had happened. He was simply allowing me the privilege of seeing it through the eyes of redemption and sonship. The moment death entered that room and overtook Hope, the Father was ready to bring His daughter into the birth of eternity. Her birth of spiritual awakening into heaven began that day. Just as the cross represents both death and life, so does every believer's crossing over. I am not trying to glorify Hope's tragic actions that day. Suicide is never the Father's will. But the moment she made a decision, Jesus made His. He chose to receive her in heaven instead of saving her for earth.

After we moved last year, I swept out the van. It was extremely emotional for me. The van was the place Hope and I last spoke to each other, and the words she spewed out in anger were running in a loop in my mind as I swept. The trauma I experienced in that van made it difficult for me to even drive it every day. Tears rolled down as I swept, realizing I was sweeping up the last residue of Hope in this place full of so many good and bad memories. As we did in her room, I was obsessing over her hair that I found on the mats as a small sign of her life. I got to the back seats and opened up the storage box on one of the sides, and found a balled-up piece of paper. I unwrapped it in curiosity to find this short note: ~~Although though we have our moments~~ *I'm glad to call you my mom. Happy 44 years young.* She had crossed out the first part of the sentence.

The last words that left her mouth that day cut at my heart and brought so much pain, guilt, regret, and question to me, wondering if she knew how much I loved her. But here was a note written three years before her passing, left in the van as if dropped from heaven to tell me how much she loved me. God had redeemed what the enemy had tried to steal in that very spot. I had swept out the van at least eight times since she wrote that note, and I had never found it.

The Father uses many ways to heal the trauma in our lives. Isabella did what came naturally for her in the moment of trauma. Since the kids were little, I had always taught them to journal their feelings. It is a healthy way to process things, and it makes it easier to find God's voice while writing. After we got to the hotel the night Hope passed, Isabella began to journal her feelings of the day:

I am sad today. My sister had an accident in the bathroom, and she is in heaven right now. She was an amazing sister. She was always there for me through the hard times. Even though we would fight a lot, she was already there for me. I cannot forget her. It is hard to go through this stuff. It hurts a lot to be hurting. I wish I could take, just take those moments back and make them last forever. She was the most kind and most helpful friend I could ever have. I wish she were here today so I can say this to her. Her name hope will be lasted in our family forever. When I am writing this note, I am bawling my eyes out. When I got off the bus, I saw an ambulance, fire truck, and police. It was hard to take this in, in my mind. When I got off the bus, tears fell as I saw my sister in the thing that they pull you on the ambulance. My heart was beating, and my chest was beating faster. When I got in the neighbor's house, I cried. Then when my family came to pick me up, they had to break the news. My sister was in heaven. I could not believe this was happening. In there, I stood crying my eyes out in my dad's sweatshirt. All the church family and our friends were there to support us through the hardship and the difficulties. It does not feel good when your life is broken down inside, and this is the first experience that I have had in my life of someone dying. Hope will be in my life forever. And someday, I will get to see her in heaven. I pray that when she died, it did not hurt and that she will stay forever in our family's heart.

If you are struggling with trauma of any kind, you can find your own heaven's perspective to replace or erase your experience. It does not make what happened okay or make it disappear, but it helps our minds latch onto another perspective and bring the roadway of resurrection and Hope.

My husband went through a therapy called MDR. They use this therapy method on veterans with PTSD. I don't know a lot about it since I myself did not clinically go through it. Nor am I telling you to go through it necessarily. But it did help my husband tremendously. What I do understand about it, though, is that you are taken through a situation that has caused your trauma and PTSD while at the same time having to be in the present

sense of humor. Even her own devotionals are full of hope, life, and truth. How could she have lost this battle to the enemy?

I will never know exactly what she was thinking in that very hour or last minute of her life, but I have come to this conclusion: Jesus knew. He was ready to rescue her, just not in the way I wanted or thought He would.

While searching, I found the last devotional Hope had read in her Bible App a week before her passing. She had highlighted this scripture in that devotional:

> Now the serpent was more cunning than any beast of the field which the Lord God had made. And he said to the woman, "Has God indeed said, 'You shall not eat of every tree of the garden'?" And the woman said to the serpent, "We may eat the fruit of the trees of the garden; but of the fruit of the tree which is in the midst of the garden, God has said, 'You shall not eat it, nor shall you touch it, lest you die.' "Then the serpent said to the woman, "You will not surely die. For God knows that in the day you eat of it your eyes will be opened, and you will be like God, knowing good and evil." So when the woman saw that the tree was good for food, that it was pleasant to the eyes, and a tree desirable to make one wise, she took of its fruit and ate. She also gave to her husband with her, and he ate. Then the eyes of both of them were opened, and they knew that they were naked; and they sewed fig leaves together and made themselves coverings."
>
> Genesis 3:1–7 (NKJV)

The enemy tempts us all to partake of the forbidden fruit in many ways. He tenaciously finds our weakest links and offers our soul fulfillment of longings that brings temporary relief but leads to death and not life. Hope longed to be accepted and to fit in. Her self-image made her feel rejected and afraid to expose her deepest struggles. As so many of us do, she searched to find acceptance in those who suffered from the same thing. She searched for someone to share her thoughts with that would not judge her. We found out that three of Hope's closest friends struggled with suicidal thoughts. We knew of one beautiful young lady's struggle prior to Hope's passing but did not know at all about the other two. I even tried to have her distance herself from one friendship, knowing it would not be healthy for Hope to be close to someone who also suffered from self-image issues. Similar to an "alcoholic's best friend is another alcoholic," I didn't think this relationship would be healthy for either girl. Satan feeds upon the fertile ground like this, and the friendship gives them temporary comfort and acceptance but not deliverance or help. The relationship makes the problem worse. We believe this was a huge issue for Hope. She was spending time with others who came into agreement with Satan's fruit for her life and theirs, just like Adam and Eve. Friendships have incredible weight in what we think and do because they connect our souls. They mean everything to a teenager who is trying to hear God's voice above their own or Satan's. I certainly do not place blame on any of these girls or anyone else in her life. We are all broken in some way, and Satan knows exactly how to dangle that fruit in front of us. But for parents who are reading about our journey, I pray you receive an understanding of how important the right friendships are for your children.

I also know that social platforms make it incredibly difficult to monitor relationships, especially those like our seventeen-year-old daughter's. Social media and platforms are absolutely Satan's fruit dangled before this generation. A child or youth will look at one picture where they were not included, one post of what someone did, a photoshopped, perfect image that they can never look like, and be negatively affected. Without one word spoken, thoughts are flooding through their heads every single minute as they scroll down the pages of "big techs" offerings. In the documentary "Social Dilemma," it is explained how many of the top players who helped invent and distribute social media control their viewers. It tells stories of how much control these "big tech" companies have over thoughts and actions. Every single parent should sit down and watch this with their children before allowing them to have a phone or engage on social platforms. This world is controlled by Satan, who would like to keep an entire generation controlled by emotions. According to the "Social Dilemma" documentary, the suicide rate has significantly increased since 2009, when social media was first introduced on smartphones. In 2017, the suicide rate for kids ages 10–14 went up 151 percent, and for youth ages 15–19, it went up 70 percent. Emotions are a gift from God but should always be subject to the truth of God's Word and the Spirit of the Father within us. Kids, youth, and even young adults are not equipped to handle the amount of false reality the world is throwing at them. Even though we tried to control Hope's exposure and engagement on social media, the industry knows very well it has a life of its own. In many ways, we do not control it. It controls us. I have no doubt the social platform manipulation of emotional enticement and torment had a great effect on Hope.

We do not believe, nor did the detective that did the investigation believe, that Hope thought she was going to die that day. Most who attempt suicide do not die on the first attempt. It was a cry for help, but also the Accuser's voice at the tree of life, tempting Hope to try what he had to offer. Satan said to Eve, "You will surely not die." This is a lie Satan whispers into the ear of so many. It does not have to be suicide. It could be drugs, adultery, alcohol, or anything that separates us from the will of the Father in our lives. Everything we do in life begins with a thought. The thought can come from someone else or our own flesh, but either way, it will be life or death to our soul. Hope had allowed the thoughts of her enemy to take root, and she took a bite of what he was giving her. One bite, one thought at a time, Satan began convincing Hope that she was not good enough, pretty enough, smart enough, loved enough, and that she had no friends. Satan preyed on her low self-esteem. Because she did not understand her identity in Christ, she believed that everyone thought of her the same way she thought of herself. When it comes down to the root of it, she did not fully understand and walk in her identity in the Father.

That leads me to the next "why." Why didn't Jesus save her? After having my first three children, I grew in the Lord expeditiously. I had suffered through so much loss in my life, and my heart longed for the Father to fill every void. As I grew, it was in my walk as a mother. I was blessed not to have to work after having Hope, so I spent my days studying the Word, doing ministry, and praying. I prayed daily for my family. My daily heart-filled prayer was pleading the blood of Jesus over my family and keeping us from all temptation and evil. I asked for us to be given Godly wisdom and understanding and allowing us to be the light and salt to the earth, bearing much fruit for the Kingdom of God. I constantly worshipped and spent time in intercession for my children and husband. I had anointed the house and each bedroom many times in the past sixteen years. I had fought in the spirit realm when I knew my kids were going through something. I even remember one day going into Hope's room and breaking the spirit of death over her bed. I had no idea if she was suicidal, but I did know of some of her struggles, and I prayed as the Father led me.

The questions repeated themselves in my mind: "So WHY, GOD? What did I do wrong? Why did you allow Satan to steal my child from me? I prayed your Word! Isn't it supposed to go and do what it was sent to do? Why didn't you keep her from all temptation and evil? Where was the God of Abraham? Where was the God of Daniel? Where was the God of Lazarus? Was He not the same God as the one in my Bible? I served you just like all of these men."

The answers did not come right away, and the pain I felt was betrayal from the Lord. I went back in forth, blaming myself for not fighting enough spiritually for her and blaming the Father for not saving her as He promised in His Word to do. But in a moment of sheer pain and anguish, He answered my "why."

"My child, Oh, but I did answer your prayer. I made a choice that day to receive her in heaven instead of saving her for earth to keep her from all temptation and evil. Not for one more second or moment can Satan touch her again. She is safe with me. No more torment, no more temptation, no more lies. I have honored your faithful prayers for her."

An unimaginable amount of gratitude flooded my heart that the Father had taken her home. For the first time since her passing, I could worship the God I served freely with no reservation or hindrance. His ways are not ours, and although I would have rather Him answer my prayer my own way, I had to abandon to His way. We, as Christians, sometimes pray prayers with the expectation of how that prayer should and will be answered. Nobody, especially us, would have considered the Father answering in the way He did. But isn't He God? Isn't He sovereign to decide? The Father knew what was coming in her life far greater than I did, and I must trust that her life was better spent in heaven at that point than down on earth. It was as if He was saying to me that Satan was not going to get this one. She had been fought for, and enough was enough! Had she lived, we do not know the kind of hell she would have lived with. We do not know how far down the road darkness would have taken her. Would I have walked in fear every time we had a slight disagreement, or if she had a bad day, thinking, "This might be it?" I am not saying I am in any way happy that she took her life. She left this earth too young, and it aborted some of the greatest pleasures the Father had reserved for her on this earth. But the moment she made her decision, the Father made His. I must rest in the peace that He knows what is best.

As the "whys" came, so did my wrestling with the predestination and sovereignty of God. Who was this God I served? Does He know it all? Was it predestined before Hope was born to end this away? Does He truly know how it is going to end for us before we even live? What kind of love is it to create a child, knowing that they are going to kill themselves in torment?

I cannot tell you I have all the biblical scholars' answers, but what I am going to tell you is from spending time at the cliff of "whys" with the Father. I had to abandon what I thought I knew and discover Him as someone who would have to partake of His cup of suffering. There is a partnership and, at times, war between the perfect will of the Father and the sovereign law of humanity's choice. His perfect will was that Adam and Eve would not eat of its fruit, but He allowed them to do so. When Adam and Eve disobeyed, sin, evil, and sickness, entered the earth. God cannot go back on His own laws and principles for His kingdom and earth. So why does God allow evil and sin to hurt people? If He intervened, making a choice of no avail, He would be going against the laws of His own kingdom. He is not a man who would lie. His character is true and holy. He cannot rebel against Creation's laws; it is not in Him. To do so would mean to abort the heart of humanity. He would not have the pleasure of having an authentic relationship with His children. Instead, it would be a forced, religious, heartless relationship. I heard Steven Furtick recently make this profound statement that brought truth to my "whys" of sovereignty and predestination, "God is *always* in control, yet He does not always *take* control." The Father took His hands off the wheel with Adam and Eve, and He does at times with you and me. He refuses to take control of the hearts and souls of His children in greater hope that His heart would become their heart by choice, not by mandate.

Here is where the hope is embedded. Here is the victory. Satan does *not* win in the end. We *always* get the victory. Whether evil, sin, or a fallen world causes us to die and leave this earth, it has no effect on our ability to live eternally in the Kingdom. We only need to accept the free gift of salvation. This is the hope of the cross. Jesus, in the garden and even at Lazarus' tomb, took upon Himself the weight of all suffering as a result of the Garden of Eden. We all must face evil, sin, and death. No one is exempt. But if we take upon ourselves the blood and flesh of Jesus, He has made a way of escape. He *is* the way of our escape. This is the ultimate joy of the cross. It is not just about a Savior, but it is the *only* way to victory over death.

God did not *will* Hope to die, but He *allowed* it. He took His hands off the wheel. That is the difference between the permissive will of the Father and the perfect will. It was not the Father's perfect will for her to take her life, but it was His *permissive* will. He did not intervene, but He fulfilled His promise to her and rescued her from the enemy of death.

After Hope's passing, many people wanted to comfort us. Many words were spoken out of love, and their thoughts were deeply appreciated. However, one of the things spoken many times was how the Father "knew this was going to happen." That struck me each time at the pit of my stomach. How could this be... but how could it not be? I did not rebuke their explanation, but I wrestled with it until the Father made a roadway out of my "why." I know what they were saying was part truth. Certainly, He knew the torment of her mind far more than we did. He knew her thoughts about ending her life, and He knew the lies Satan was throwing at her. That day when I was in the basement, He was right there with her and knew that temptation was overcoming her. He was right there when she did what she did. However, I do not believe that when I opened my arms and held Hope in my hands and heart for the first time, the Father was looking at her and saying, "This one is going to commit suicide at seventeen."

I do not think He creates any human being and sees their sin, but instead, He sees their full perfect potential as a child of God. He sees His promises and future within their eyes, and He knows the plans He has for them: plans to prosper them, plans not to give them harm but a hope and a future (Jeremiah 29:11). He is well aware that they will endure suffering. There will be trauma, and they will wrestle with the evil one who comes to steal, kill, and destroy. But, the Father looks at the victory of the cross. He sees each one of us by the blood and resurrection of His son Jesus, and He believes we can overcome. At what point did that change for Hope? Was it years, months, days, or just hours before? I do not know. But I do know that she was not predestined to have a defeated life.

Ever since Hope was a baby, I declared this truth told to me by the Father when He saved her life in the womb: "You will be Hope to the Hopeless." Hope had a calling. Just like Jeremiah, I believe the Father calls us all from our mother's womb (Jeremiah 1:5). He is a generational God that looks far past the chasm of death. He looks into eternity. One generation to another, He calls us to bring His kingdom on earth and for His will to be done, as it is in heaven (Matthew 6:10). If from the time a child is in their mother's womb, their destination is sin, destruction, taking their own life at seventeen, then what hope is there?

The Father has infused in each one of us a calling that supersedes this life into the next. Hope's calling to be "Hope to the hopeless" did not end when she died. Her calling did not begin here, and it did not end here either. At the cliff of my "whys," I have asked the Father how Hope could still be "hope to the hopeless" in light of what she has done. How can her life represent hope when hopelessness took her life? Again, the Father asked me to see with *His* eyes, to look past where I was standing. As I looked upon the horizon, I began to see circumstances, situations, and events around her death and those preceding it that widened my view. Things aren't about just one person. There is always a bigger picture. To be a child of God is to be a part of something greater than yourself.

The week of Hope's passing, they were doing a "Hope Week" at her high school. She did not attend the school anymore since she was online, but it was still her school. The events were organized by the "Hope Squad." The group was formed by an organization called "Grantushope.org." They go into the schools to focus on suicide prevention. The very day she died was "sunflower day," which was her favorite flower. Everything they do for the week is in yellow. That was Hope's favorite color. At the entrance of the building were big letters that spelled out "Hope." Because COVID hit and the schools shut down, that word stayed up there from January to September of 2020. I do not think she purposely coincided her death with this event or even knew that it was going on. However, the Father knew, and I think He was speaking to us through it. Hope's story would be used as a voice to break the spirit of suicide off a generation, just like this event does.

I was beginning to feel a stirring for the good and glory in our story. I was ready to start abandoning the "whys" and move toward resurrection and hope.

I used to believe that in heaven, at least I would know the answer to the big "whys," but now I think I will never know some of them because it will not matter in heaven. God's glory will fulfill all the "whys."

In her book *The Louder Song: Listening for Hope in the Midst of Lament*, Aubrey Sampson said it best: "In our deepest grief, we don't lament to find answers. We lament to stop searching for them. We lament to be still in the unanswerable."

Here I was. I had the courage to walk up to the edge of my cliff of "whys" and lay it all down at the altar before my Father, and the mountain before me became a roadway to resurrection, life, and Hope.

I abandoned my thoughts of needing to know all the answers to why Hope did what she did. I abandoned my thoughts that the Father should have honored my prayers and answered them the way I wanted. I abandoned my thought that God predestined the outcome of Hope's life, making human choice of no avail. I abandoned my thought that her calling was over at her death on this earth.

I worshipped at the Altar of "Whys" to the Father who fulfills all the questions in eternity. I worshipped at the Altar of "Whys" to the sovereign God who chooses to answer His word in His way, not ours. I worshipped the Father, who is not a God who lies or goes back on His kingdom laws or ways. I worshipped at the Altar of "Whys" to a perfect Father who will fulfill His calling in Hope, even from heaven.

Chapter 9: The Cliff of the Unknown

As the time came to the one-year mark of Hope's passing, I heard the Father gently whispering to me to come to the edge of the cliff of our unknown present and future. The life that we thought we had was not the life we were now living. We had to find our footing again, our new "normal." But there were and still are so many unknowns. As I moved tenderly and cautiously to the edge of the cliff, I feared leaving my life shattered on the raw, exposed, jagged rocks of suffering and brokenness. I did not want to still be broken or shattered, but if I walked away from that season of my life, I would risk leaving the spot where Hope once was in our lives and in our future. In a way, the suffering and journey in the pieces of a shattered life felt comforting and normal.

What I have learned in speaking with those in deep grief is this is a common emotion. You may feel you are in this place today. If we are not careful, we can get stuck in this place, unable to move forward. I want to encourage you that as you read how the Father used many different circumstances to gently move me forward, He will move you too. But you have to be willing to embrace those gentle nudges and have the courage to go beyond the edge. Jesus won't let you go. His plans for you are *still* good. When you have spent what seems like a lifetime creating "your world," and in one moment, it falls to the ground, fear becomes your biggest hindrance to a life being created once again.

As laughter began to fill our home again on occasions, I had a quick nudge of guilt. Our daughter is gone… what are we doing laughing again? Faithanna got engaged on Mother's

Day weekend, with a wedding expected in June 2022. Preparing to be the mother of the bride gave me hope, excitement, and something to look forward to, but then a wave of sorrow would hit as I looked back from the edge and realized her sister would not be coming with us on this journey. Not only will she not be a part of her sister's wedding, but she will also never get married. I will never help plan *her* wedding. Samuel graduated from Christ for the Nations in Dallas, Texas. He graduated from Market Place Ministry and hopes to operate his own Chick-Fil-A. We are so incredibly proud of him, but with his graduation, we were reminded of another graduation we were supposed to be attending this year. Hope would have graduated from high school in the spring of 2021. I remember praying that their graduation ceremonies would not overlap. I wish now I would have had to deal with that challenge. Looking at the graduation posts of her friends has been extremely difficult. We found out that Samuel and his wife Jasmine are expecting, and we are going to have our first grandchild. Hope would have made a loving aunt. Hope deferred makes the heart sick.

But here is where I refuse to stay. I cannot stop now. I must take my walk to the edge of the "Cliff of the Unknown," where the Father is waiting to show me His kingdom perspective. I would have never imagined that in less than two years of Hope's passing, we would have one child engaged and one expecting a baby. The reality of life is full of unknowns. Each day can bring joy and sorrow. Life on earth is meant to be experienced, explored, and lived to the fullness of the Father's potential and purpose for us. But life lived on earth is not the one lived in heaven. Things like graduations, personal achievements, and even getting married and having children are and will continue to be incredible accomplishments and joyous occasions full of purpose on earth. But these are *earthly* experiences and dreams fulfilled, not those of heaven. I can choose to look at Hope through the unfulfilled dreams of earth, or I can choose to see her graduate through the mercy seat of Christ to the banquet table of our King and His kingdom. Now, she is married to Christ. Her views tower over the Colorado mountains, where she wanted to go for her graduation vacation. Standing in heaven, would she look back in sorrow on what she did not do or accomplish on earth? I do not think so. Only those of us left on earth do that. I miss her daily, but I hear her voice beckon me to look beyond the edge of the unknown and dream, live, breathe, and find hope again. If she does not feel sorrow for unfulfilled accomplishments on that side of heaven, we should not either. I cannot stay in what *wasn't*. What *wasn't* will keep me from embracing what *is* and what *is to be*. Here is a poem Hope wrote at age twelve. The Father was speaking to her then, and now He is speaking through her to us:

FOCUS YOUR EYES AHEAD

Don't look back, little one

Focus your eyes ahead

You're stronger than your past

The past is our weakness

The future is your superpower

Oh! Little one,

Don't you see

It can only get better

Just focus your eyes

Ahead

—Hope Noelle White

Hope is safe now. She is experiencing eternal and constant glory and joy. But here on earth, I have a family that needs me.

I have two beautiful girls still at home, and they deserve for me to be present with them. I still need to pray for them, love them, teach them, take care of them, laugh with them, dream with them, and hope with them. Jason deserves the best of me as well. We still have a full life to live together. We need each other to be in the present moment together. Life does move on. It must. How long can you stand between two different lifetimes?

In my wrestling, I asked the Father to give me a revelation, or Rhema word, to hold on to for my soul. I needed to know that Hope—our Hope and His—would be found in the "forward." His word did not give me the answers to the deeper questions of the communion between earth and heaven where Hope lived. As the mama who carried Hope for nine months, bone of my bone, flesh of my flesh... I needed to know that we were somehow still connected. I needed confirmation that our relationship on earth still mattered. I could not bear the thought that it was all just gone.

Several days later, out of the blue, Jason called me and asked me to pick up Chick-Fil-A for him on my way home. I was not thinking of my request to the Lord that day, but the Father was. I drove up, rolled down my window, and the young man asked for the name on the order. When I said "Alicia," he asked me to spell it for him. I did, and he repeated my name and spelling. In the years I have frequented Chick-fil-A, no one has ever asked me to spell my name. He took my order and kindly told me to pull up to the next gentleman, who would verify my order and give me a receipt. I drove up, and the gentleman said in a very matter-of-fact voice, "Hope." I hesitated, as you can imagine. I said, "Excuse me, what did you say?" He then repeated it in a slightly different way, "Your order is for Hope, right?" I began to cry. After maybe twenty seconds, I mustered up enough voice to say, "No, my order was for Alicia." He talked into his lapel mic and explained to them that the order he had for my white Sienna was "Hope." After they answered, which I could not hear, he told me that he could not figure it out either. He said I would have to go around to the window, and they would get it straightened out. When I got to the window, the order was under "Alicia."

This was truly my "supernatural" sign. The Father answered me in such a way that I had no doubt it was from Him. Remember, the gentleman had me spell and say my name when he took my order. There was no question that he might have misunderstood me. After I pulled away that day, I heard the Lord speak into my spirit: "The veil is thinner than you think between heaven and earth. Hope is closer than you think. Wherever you go, you will order hope into the room." I had my release to abandon the unknown present and future and continue on the roadway to resurrection and hope.

From that day on, I had a new sense of confidence that Hope was coming along on our journey. She was not left behind in the shambles of our past, but she would somehow be part of our future.

This revelation opened my heart for the first time to ministry, but not as it had been. I felt the leading of the Spirit to mark the exact night Hope passed with a message to her generation, many of them being her friends at our home church. I knew the Father was asking me to share our story, not just the tragic message, but the hope in it for a generation. I began to dig into her devotionals for the first time, and what I found was incredibly amazing. I found her voice in her peers. Her journals were full of hope and truth. I knew they had to become part of my message. On Wednesday, January 27, 2021—a year to the day of her passing—I simply became her voice. It was a snowy Ohio night. The roads were not very good, yet the turnout of students was large. I looked into the eyes of more than sixty kids, and I saw my Hope. Tears rolled down their faces as they listened to every word. You could hear a pin drop. As I started the altar ministry time, I heard myself say these Spirit-led words: "I am ordering Hope into this room." Sometimes when we have an encounter with the Father, He partially unpacks what it means for us. I knew when I said those words in front of the youth and parents that night that it was part of what the Father was saying and doing through the Chick-Fil-A encounter. As I became a voice of hope and my daughter, the Lord was giving me the authority to order Hope into the room. At the end of the evening, many received hope as they encountered the Father's love. Families were healed as parents embraced their teens and young adults in a moment of transparency and brokenness. Our counselor came and made herself available to the families after the service. Her table was packed full of kids and parents for over forty-five minutes afterward.

I realized that night that it was time to see with the Father's eyes the plans He had for us. There will still be uncertain days, but it is time to embrace the unknown and stand before a generation to bring the message of hope *and* Hope's message. It was time to break off the spirit of suicide and partner with Jesus to see a generation come into their identities as sons and daughters.

Again, here, it is noteworthy how the Father's timing in our lives paralleled what was happening in the world during the COVID crisis. There are some statistics finding suicides up over 200 percent since the beginning of the pandemic. The isolation, hopelessness, death-focused culture, and ideologies of untruth were and are fertile ground for the spirit of death to bring its fruit to kill and destroy a generation. The message of hope and Hope's message could never be more needed than now.

We found a letter Hope wrote in 2017 tucked away under an old email address that she had not used in a long time. She had written it in cursive, took a picture of it, and emailed it to herself. The letter was hard to read from the picture, and we never found the original in her devotionals, but Isabella typed out what it said for us. I believe the letter you are about to read was a prophetic letter from the Father to Hope. Hope wrote it down and gave it to at least one of her friends. Isabella printed out this letter and drew the picture at the bottom. I was sitting on a bench waiting for her to finish horse therapy one day when I saw that she had put the letter in her school folder. When I looked at the picture she drew, the Father spoke this scripture to me: "Listen carefully: Unless a grain of wheat is buried in the ground, dead to the world, it is never any more than a grain of wheat. But if it is buried, it sprouts and reproduces itself many times over" (John 12:24, MSG). Hope would produce far more fruit in heaven than she would ever from earth. This was the justice and recompense for a life to Jesus the devil thought he had. I remembered the words I spoke at her funeral, "She is a word sent from heaven to earth. Her purpose will not fall to the ground but is eternal and everlasting and will continue to manifest and bear fruit through everyone who was touched by her life. God's word will not return void. If you have been touched by her sweet and precious life, you now have a responsibility to carry on Hope. Hope for the Father's peace. Hope for the Father's love. Hope for the Father's freedom. Hope for an abundant life. Hope for healing. Hope for deliverance. Hope for joy. Hope for eternal life. Hope for hell to be made smaller… and heaven to expand its borders.

"Listen to my words, children and youth. Satan will pay for what he has done, and God will have His vengeance."

Hope's Original Letter

May 25th 2017

If your reading this, well I hope it helps you, or I hope that it will at least put a smile on your face. I just wanted to tell you how beautiful you are. I want you to know that if your reading this then you have helped me in my life termediously. Let me tell you something your one of a kind. There is no one... Absolutely no one else like you, yes beautiful you are so so so special. you might not feel like it right now but believe me you are. So many people care about you including me. your not here by accident. you are going to do so much to change the world. you have a purpose and a destiny! In order to fulfill your purpose you must tell yourself, "No matter how hard it is, or how hard it gets, I'm going to make it." It does not matter what other people think or say. you never need to let other people's thoughts or actions control your life. Don't ever invest in things or people that don't invest back in you. Only invest in people that invest back in you. Many things will not go your way in life, But maybe seeing what will is the best adventure in life. Also remember your past does not define you. you can't start the next chapter of your life if you always re-read the last one. you need to move on to bigger and better things your Joy in life is one of the biggest things that matters in life. please brethe and look at the positives in life. Happiness CAN be found even in the darkest if times, Even when no-one is around. So beautiful remember your worth it and your so so so special. Dont forget to smile! So many people care about you!

Hope's letter reads:

If you are reading this, well, I hope it helps you, or I hope that it will at least put a smile on your face. I just wanted to tell you how beautiful you are. I want you to know that if you are reading this, then you have helped me in my life tremendously. Let me tell you something you are one of a kind. There is no one... absolutely no one else like you. Yes, beautiful, you are so special. You might not feel like it right now but believe me, you are. So many people care about you, including me. You're not here by accident. You are going to do so much to change the world. You have a purpose and a destiny. In order to fulfill your purpose, you must tell yourself, "No matter how hard it is or how hard it gets, I'm going to make it." It does not matter what other people think or say. You never need to let other people's thoughts or actions control your life. Do not ever invest in things or people that don't invest back in you. Only invest in people that invest back in you. Many things will not go your way in life, but maybe seeing what will is the best adventure in life. Also, remember your past does not define you. You cannot start the next chapter of your life if you always relive the last one. You need to move on to bigger and more important things. Your joy in life is one of the biggest things that matters in life. Happiness CAN be found even in the darkest times, even when no one is around. So beautiful, you're worth it, and you're so, so, so special. Do not forget to smile! So many people care about you!!!

Isabella's drawing underneath the typed letter

Hope was not buried, but planted into the deep, rich soil of the kingdom to produce the fruit of heaven on earth.

That very night we went to church to worship with a guest worship leader and minister named Eddie James. For years, I had been "that" one who would be at the altar in expressive worship on any given Sunday. But after Hope passed, worship took an incredible sacrifice, and the liberty and freedom were just not there. The altar had become a place where our daughter's lifeless body had been laid to rest at her memorial service. For months after, it was hard just to go to a service because of that vision, but eventually, I was able to put those thoughts aside. But going to the altar and worshipping where she laid… I was unable to do. But on this night, I heard the voice of the Lord ask of me, "Will you go and worship in the very spot your daughter was laid to rest?" My heart jumped out of my chest just thinking about doing this. I made up my mind that if the Father confirmed or opened a door, I would go. A couple of songs later, Eddie encouraged people to get out of their seats and go to the altar to worship. Although I was afraid, I decided to go up.

As I worshipped in that spot, my eyes caught one of the stickers our church had placed at the altar to identify "social distancing" designated spots for people to stand during the pandemic. These stickers were yet another parallel of Hope's passing. Our pastor has a church theme or focus each year. Before the day of January 29, it was already decided the theme for the first half of the year would be "Hope Lives Here." If that wasn't enough, the sticker that was at my feet as I worshipped that night said: "Hope Lives Here!" It was a stark contradiction to her lifeless body that had been in that very spot last January.

The more I worshipped, the more I felt both the hope of the Lord and the life of my sweet Hope. I heard again the voice of the Lord: "Tonight, you ordered Hope into this room through your worship. I will break off the spirit of suicide upon my sons and daughters."

As Eddie James ministered, he spoke about how the Father was delivering people, despite the rise in the suicide rate of our country. He testified how he saw those who were cutters and those who struggled with suicidal thoughts breaking free this year as he traveled the nation. His altar call, though, was not for that specifically. As the night drew to a close, I felt confused as to what the Lord was saying to me and what Eddie's message meant. He was on the platform giving his last words of encouragement when a young lady, who was one of Hope's friends, came up to the front and grabbed his attention. Immediately, it reminded me of the woman with the issue of blood as she reached up on the stage and almost grabbed his ankles. As he bent down, she whispered in his ear. I knew what she was saying. I had known her struggle with suicide, and Hope did too. People tend to find friends who are of like spirit for comfort and acceptance, but teenagers do not realize that this can cause more harm than good. This beautiful young lady not only had already been suicidal, but now was struggling even more due to Hope's death. I immediately ran to her to pray as Eddie called on spiritual mothers to cover her. I knew with everything that was within me that the Father was going to break the spirit of suicide in her. Many others came forward that night too. At one point, I remember yelling out "Hope" three times. It startled even me. But I knew it was not me being weird and calling down my daughter. It was the anointing and authority in me calling down the hope of Christ. That young lady messaged me a couple of days later and said in eleven years. She had never felt free from the spirit. But *that* night, she had been healed and delivered. I believe that night held the first fruit of deliverance from suicide of many to come.

After the service, we found Eddie James to speak to him in private. In a meeting room, we shared our story with him and cried together. As he began to respond and minister to us, the first words out of his mouth were John 12:24… the exact scripture the Father had given me earlier that day. I knew that was a confirmation of what happened that night. He prayed with us and declared that Hope's story would be hope to the hopeless in the nations—the very declaration that I spoke over Hope all her life. God was doing something. He was allowing our eyes to see beyond the veil of flesh and earth. But more than that, He was releasing us into our future.

That was not where the fruit of "hope" ended for my family during that week. Samuel, our son who lives in Dallas and is in his last year at Christ for the Nations, called me the day following Eddie's service. After I told him what had happened to us the night before, he began to weep as he told me that he had just had an encounter with the Holy Spirit. He awoke early for school that day. He knew the Lord had woken him up because he *never* gets up early on his own. He got up and left for school. While waiting to go into the chapel, he turned off his car, and suddenly, he began to weep uncontrollably. He pulled up his Bible app to read the scriptures, but instead of going to the home page, it went to the page of "friend." There, he saw Hope as one of his friends on the app. He clicked on her name to find her very last post in the Bible app staring back at him just ten days before her death.

YOU ARE SO LOVED

Hope's last post *ten* days before her passing

The Holy Spirit begins to speak to him these words:

If you had ten days left on this earth... what would you say? What would you do? What prayers would you fervently pray? What people would you go and talk to, and what secrets would you let out? Ten days. Jesus is not caught off guard by the ten days. Ten hours. Ten minutes. Ten seconds. He was not caught off guard when you received the phone call. He did not panic when you started asking the hard questions. Surely did not start sweating when the numbness started fading away and reality set in. He was right next to you, closer than your very breath, bigger than your deepest fear, ready to move with you through the chaos.

As he shared his encounter in a social media post, he continued to write:

My God does not move because of my circumstances; my circumstances move because of my God. She had ten days left on earth and did not even know it when she made this. What will you do with ten days left?

After posting it on social media, he went to his first class, which was on "Sonship." This class taught students how to find identity as a son or daughter of the Father. When he arrived in the classroom, no one else was there but his professor. As he walked up to him, the professor noticed that he had been crying. After being asked, Samuel told him about his strong encounter with the Holy Spirit that morning and our story of Hope. They both cried together, and the professor prayed for him. A few minutes after class had started, the professor stopped and said, "This is the day you all will become sons and daughters of God." They began to worship and minister before the Lord.

I believe Hope's last words in the app ministered directly to the heart of her brother Samuel. It was what he needed to hear that day. It wasn't just him that needed the message, but many others as well. What the Father did to and through Samuel that day was so sovereign and profound. Hope struggled to find her place as a daughter of the Father. The Father, even now, and even more so now, will use Hope to bring hope to the hopeless and break the spirit of suicide through the love of the Father. This was yet another manifestation of this truth.

The week was not over, and the Father still had more to do. Isabella had befriended a little girl at school whose mother had died several years ago. She was being raised by her father and brother in the Muslim faith. They shared their loss together, and Isabella found that this little girl, not having another female in her family, needed her encouragement. She also must have seen Jesus in her because over recess that week, she asked Isabella to lead her in a prayer to accept Him as her Savior. She got in the car that day, grinning ear to ear, to tell me all about it. The following day at lunch, the young lady asked Isabella to teach her how to pray to Jesus. Hope's story will become Isabella's testimony of what God can do in a season of suffering.

The week still had more messages from God. Faithanna received a breakthrough she desperately needed. She had been going to school for a bachelor's degree in nursing but had her nurse assistant license, so she has been working as one for a couple of years. Her job was a third shift, and that created a lot of extra stress in a season when she truly needed healing. Because of the uptick of suicidal children and the reorganization of job assignments due to COVID, Faithanna was often required to sit one-on-one with "suicide watch" patients. You can imagine what type of trauma this triggered in her. She had hit rock bottom with her job and desperately needed a change. That very week, she got a new job that moved her to the first shift and eliminated all of the extra stressors. Although her story did not sound as dramatic as the other ones in our family, it was exactly what *her* spirit and soul needed.

"But as for you, you meant evil against me; *but* God meant it for good, in order to bring it about as *it is* this day, to save many people alive" (Genesis 50:20, NKJV).

Satan can try… and he will… to stop God's kingdom from multiplying and His will to be done on earth as it is in heaven—but he will not succeed. It may look like defeat, but for those who serve the Lord, the Father will find a way to use it all for His good and glory. Satan thought ending Hope's life on earth would end her purpose and ours. But her death will only increase what we do for the Kingdom. Satan has tried to keep us in a state of hopelessness as a family and individually, but God will turn what Satan meant for evil, and souls will be saved, delivered, and set free in the name of Jesus!

As I began to feel a nudging from the Father to start sharing with youth and use our testimony to set others free, I began to volunteer in our youth ministry at church. I would often pray for the youth during the altar ministry time. One particular night a young lady came up, and I prayed for her. I don't even remember now exactly what I spoke over her. But the next Wednesday, she came looking for me during worship. She asked if she could hug me, and of course, I said yes. As she embraced me for a long time, she told me how thankful she was for my prayer and how the last week she had received freedom in a lot of areas in her life. She was full of hope. As we pulled away from each other, I asked her name so I could continue to pray for her. She looked me in the eyes and said, "My name is Hope." I was overwhelmed with emotions. She was new to our church, so she had no idea about our story. As I walked away from her, the Father again spoke to me, "There are young ladies just like your Hope everywhere that are looking for freedom and healing." Since then, we have had many opportunities to minister to youth and college kids. The sound of weeping fills the room as the silence of shame and lies of the enemy are broken, but also the sound of the God of hope rushing in to heal, deliver, and bring life.

At the edge of the cliff of the unknown, I have found purpose and peace for what I could not see. My abandonment brought me to worship and worship to resurrection and Hope. There will be moments and even days of sorrow, but my feet are planted firmly on the path the Father has chosen for me and my family. He has made beauty out of our ashes. As Hope's passing drew a line of demarcation in the sands of our lives—a before and after—the Father was drawing another line of "before and after." Before, I was shattered into a million pieces, hopeless, with no future to hold onto. After, now coming into view, is a faint line of healing, restoration, resurrection, and hope. Jesus was slowly removing the cup of suffering from my hand and filling me with purpose from the pain.

Maybe you are not at this moment right now. You feel stuck, and you see no hope for your future. Grief and suffering have many stages. It's okay not to be able to see the future, much less the present. But I want to encourage you to intentionally take time, at least once a week, if not more, to seek the Father about your future. It will help you not to stay where you are forever. Find a cozy and comfortable place to sup with Jesus awhile, dream, discover the possibilities, and allow Him to speak into your heart, not about your suffering, but about His plans He has for you. Eventually, as you purposively take the time to do this, Jesus will take the cup of suffering from your hand and replaces it will a cup of joy, purpose, and life once again.

We walk in death in many ways during our lives. For some, it's in sin. For some, it's their own battle with sickness, but for some, it is sorrow and grief that sucks the life out of us. This song best describes what the Father has done in me as I have abandoned myself to the cliffs of suffering and drank from the cup, daring to believe there was more in my forward.

Here I was. I had the courage to walk up to the edge of my Cliff of the "Unknown" and lay it all down at the altar before my Father, and the mountain before me became a roadway to resurrection, life, and Hope.

I abandoned my thoughts that life would move on without Hope. I abandoned the lies of the enemy that made me think that her purpose, and even mine, were gone. I abandoned my fears about my future.

I worshipped at the Altar of the "Unknown" to the Father, who brings hope and His goodness to every place of suffering. I worshipped at the altar of the "Unknown" to Jesus, who tore the veil of separation between earth and eternity. I worshipped at the Altar of the "Unknown" to Jesus, the God of the supernatural who makes beauty from ashes. I worshipped at the Altar of the "Unknown" to a Father who opened my eyes to see heaven's perspective so the unknown would become known.

CHAPTER 10: THE GOODNESS OF THE FATHER

"*I would have lost heart,* unless I had believed That I would see the goodness of the Lord In the land of the living. Wait on the Lord; Be of good courage, And He shall strengthen your heart; Wait, I say, on the Lord!" (Psalm 27:13–14, NKJV).

There were moments along the last two-year journey when I could not see the goodness of the Lord in the land of the living. In fact, even saying the words "God is good" was very difficult at times. But the more courage I had to step to the edge of the cliffs, my perspective transformed. I began to pray every single day for my family and myself. "Father, bind to us your kingdom perspective, that we might see, hear, feel, and think all things through your lenses." The longer I set my gaze on the goodness of the Father, the more strength I had to wake up and face another day. The journey has been long and filled with emotions of longing, loneliness, grief, anger, regret, and at times, hopelessness. But as I have chosen to persevere and invite Jesus into my journey of grief and suffering, and drink from the cup of suffering with Him, I have also found places of healing, joy, laughter, peace, comfort, and hope. I have started to see His hand and His perspective on all things. The veil is truly so thin, and the Father is just waiting for us to see with His eyes and a heart of abandonment. His love is so wide and so deep that death has no power over it. The purest definition of hope is the anticipation of obtaining and experiencing the goodness of the Lord in our lives. It's a sense of deep acknowledgment that in all the pain and suffering life brings, the goodness of the Lord will prevail. Hope, an anticipation of the goodness of the Lord, gives us strength to go on and move forward when we feel like we can't take another step. He loves to give us "kisses from heaven" to remind us of this daily.

I have shared many of these "kisses from heaven," sweet reminders of the goodness of God already. But as I come to a close, I will share a few more. Two testimonies showed that He remembered our grieving hearts that begged to share life with our sweet Hope again. His goodness doesn't disappoint. Our family, minus Jason, who could not go, had just spent a few days in Dallas celebrating Samuel's graduation. I was driving us from Dallas to a little town in Arkansas where my extended family lives. Isabella needed to go to the restroom, and we drove for miles without any place to stop. Finally, we saw signs of a truck stop at the next exit. As we got off at the exit, I touched base with Jason for the day with a text. He happened to look on Life360, an app that shows the location of each family member via their phone. Of all the places we could have stopped, this was the place the Father had given us: the town of Hope.

It was simply a kiss from heaven, knowing that as I move forward, being present to my kids and family still on this earth, Hope is with us. His goodness is all around us; we just must be willing to look and wait for Him.

Isabella went on a mission trip to Mexico last summer. Hope has been on this same mission trip to Mexico twice. She absolutely loved it. Many who had gone with her said Hope seemed to be filled with joy and freedom as she chased the kids around and loved on them at the orphanage. In lieu of flowers at her funeral, we asked for donations for this orphanage. With the money the orphanage received, they planted a tree in Hope's honor on the property.

As Isabella was getting ready to go to this same orphanage, she was asked to prepare her personal testimony to share at some point on the trip. At the end of her testimony, she told everyone she wanted God to show her that Hope was nearby as she herself walked the same steps that her sister had walked while there.

A good friend who was chaperoning was with Isabella and had also been with Hope on one of her trips. It was a tradition for those who spent the day serving the kids to have their picture taken with them. As the chaperon took a picture of Isabella with one of the sweet girls, she had remembered taking one of Hope and this same little girl four years previously. She looked back in her history of pictures and found the pic.

This was our manifestation of the goodness of the Lord in the land of the living. These pictures were taken *exactly* four years apart, on *the same exact date*, with the *same precious little girl*. The picture on the right is Isabella, and the picture on the left is Hope. Only God could have orchestrated this. His goodness ran after us and answered the prayers of a little sister and a mom and dad in our journey of suffering. Hope is with us, and she will not be forgotten.

You can trust that in a world of darkness, evil, and despair, you will see the goodness of the Lord in your journey of suffering. Wait on the Lord and anticipate His goodness. You will find hope in the forward, and it will give you the strength to move on. He loves you so much. He desires to do what no one else can do for you. Wait and see.

His goodness is the *only* thing that will rescue you from the deepest pit of despair.

Less than a month before Hope passed, I bought a wall hanging with Christmas money I had received. I hung it up proudly above our fireplace at our old home. It was made up of two wooden pictures. One read *It Is Well,* and the other read *With My Soul.* It was one of the first things I saw when we dragged ourselves into the house after leaving the hospital the night she passed. My body and soul froze under the weight of the words: "It is well with my soul." How could it be? God didn't raise my daughter from the dead! Those words that night stirred up anger in me.

"Please run now to meet her and say to her, 'Is it well with you? Is it well with your husband? Is it well with the child?' And she answered, It is well'" (2 Kings 4:26, NKJV). I used to be fascinated by the faith of this mother who would say such a thing when her son was dead. Who does that? She seemed so calm and confident that Elisha was going to come and raise her child from the dead. Why was she so confident? A prophet in those days represented the voice and character of God Himself. The Holy Spirit had not been poured out, so if they were going to hear and see God, it would be through His chosen. The prophet of God had promised her a son, and this came to pass. A prophet was only as good as his word in those days. She knew if he had prophesized that she would have a son, his character and integrity rested upon him being able to raise him from the dead. She had no doubt that he would.

Like this woman, I had made room for God's presence in our home. I was blessed to be a stay-at-home mom and spent my days worshipping, praying, and ministering to the Lord in many ways. Each of our children was a gift from God. Hope's story was a story of hope. Hope was a twin, as I have already mentioned. Her twin was miscarried, but Hope survived. We named her Hope because she was our expected goodness from the Lord. She gave us hope in the God of miracles. She would be a manifestation of hope to the hopeless. But our story didn't quite end like the woman's story in the Old Testament. The prophet of God, or God Himself, didn't bring Hope back to life on this earth. My husband and I prayed that He would, but our story was not her story. Or was it? While unpacking the same wall hanging in my new home, I heard the Father begin to speak to me. "Alicia, the woman of God, spoke those words *before* her son had been raised from the dead. Before. She was confident that I would fulfill her promise one way or another. It was well with her soul. I give you that same promise. I have raised Hope from the dead and the promise I give you will come to pass." The Father knew I would need this reminder as we journeyed through our suffering. I placed it above our new fireplace, and I often look at it, whispering the words into my soul. It is well with my soul.

We are seeing the Lord's goodness all around us, and God is still the God of miracles. Hope's personal journals and story are bringing hope to the hopeless in many ways. My heart longs to have her fully alive and here with me, but it is well with my soul. My God has fulfilled His promise.

In your journey of suffering, you may wonder how you could ever say "it is well" with your soul. Maybe it is just not possible right now. But God is good and will fulfill His promises to you, one way or another. His character and integrity rest upon this.

Chapter 10: The Goodness of the Father | 129

Be confident and assured that He will do what He said. Your journey may not look like you thought it would, but He will lead you through the pain. Walk in confidence as you follow the promise keeper. You will be able to one day proclaim: "It is well."

I remember a podcast sermon someone gave me to listen to. He shared a dream he had. As he was sharing his dream, the Father used it to give me a vision of my own. This was my vision:

A father was looking out his home window to a park right across the street where he had reluctantly allowed his child to go and play. Suddenly, he saw a stranger snatch up his child. He threw open his front door and cried out with every bit of breath left in him as he ran towards his precious child and the abductor. Every part of his body, soul, and mind was demanding the stranger let go of his child. However, with each agonizing step he took, the child was farther out of his view, and hope of retrieving his child was slipping away. No matter how hard he tried, he could not reach his child.

Suddenly I heard the voice of the Father say to me:

"Not everything is as it seems. I was the one that snatched that child up. I was the abductor. It was *me*. The evil you could not see was all around Hope and seeking to destroy her. It now seeks to destroy hope in you. I saved her. She is safe with me. Turn your eyes upon me. With the same fervent longing and desperation with which you have been running to get one more glimpse, one more touch, one more moment with Hope, I want you to run after me. I have your hope. You have cried out each day of injustice and evil, but my perfect love raptured her. If you will but turn your eyes toward me and seek me with every breath, with your whole body, soul, and spirit, you will find us both. Turn your eyes upon me, look full into my wonderful face, and the things of earth will grow strangely dim in the light of my glory and grace."

I speak that to you today. Now that we have come to the end of this book, our journey has just begun. Turn your eyes upon Jesus, for He has your hope. The Father's ways are not our ways. Look through His eyes. He desires to pour His perfect love out upon you until it saturates every part of your being. You will find the one you lost in the gaze of the *one* who saved them.

When in a season of suffering, look for the Lord's presence. Wait upon the Lord. Press in to see His goodness in all things, even the worst imaginable, finding hope in the tear-soaked journey. The chasm between the cup of suffering and hope will require abandonment. Willingness to trust deeply becomes the highest form of worship.

Although the pain and grief remain, the higher perspective is the gain that earth cannot satisfy. "Take up your cross and follow me" becomes not just a Christian cliché or a duty of obedience while you expect a ram in the thicket. It is a call to lay it all down at the altars found at the cliffs of suffering and wrestling (Matthew 16:24–26). You will lose your life to gain it.

The higher walk of worship, true abandonment, will become the walk to resurrection and hope for all of us who partake in his cup of suffering in such a deep, sacrificial way. The vulnerability that leaves you before the cross naked, having given the unthinkable *all*, places a demand to be given a cloak from heaven, threaded with scarlet and draped in resurrection power and hope. When "worthy of it all" becomes your highest worship and there is nothing left in your hands, the Father's love and goodness will remain.

The road the Father has permitted for those who have endured life-altering tragic loss and suffering is the road less traveled. It is a road of anguish, but I also believe it is a road of great honor and privilege. The cup of suffering will change you forever but may change you from glory to glory if allowed. There is a strange sense of honor that the Father entrusted my family with such a cup. With every drink, we have encountered and experienced the

Father in a way few are able. There is an intimate communion with the Father and His son Jesus who knows what it is like to truly give *all*. He has entrusted us to walk the road less traveled in order to encounter His resurrection and true life found in full abandonment. We look at the cross and see both death and life. Our stories will testify to both death and life.

Along my journey, I ran across the story of Aggie, known as the girl without a country. A family went to Africa from Sweden in 1921 to evangelize in the Congo. They ran into a hindering spirit and were not permitted to enter their appointed tribe. They lived right outside the tribe, hoping for an opportunity. The only contact they ever had with the village was a young African boy who could sell them chickens and eggs twice a week. They reached that little boy and led him to Jesus. The couple had a little girl, Aina. But tragedy struck the family and the mother contracted malaria. After seventeen days, she died.

The father, struck with grief, went back to a camp where American missionaries lived safely in a commune. He visited another couple that they had known well. He gave them baby Aina and went back to Sweden, mad at God and everyone else. He cried, "God has ruined my life!" Eight months later, the couple who cared for Aina also contracted a disease and died. Aina was given over to yet another couple in the commune where she was given the Swedish name "Aggie." At age three, she traveled to South Dakota with the couple to live.

She eventually got married, and her husband was a president of a Christian university. At some point, she ran across an article from a Swedish religious magazine that shared the story of her parents. It even had a picture of her mom's grave and gave testimony of the young African boy who won his entire village to Jesus. There were over six hundred believers at the time the article was released, all because of the sacrifice of one man and woman who gave their *all* for Jesus.

Aggie eventually got to see her father before he died and shared the testimony with him. He turned his heart back to Jesus and repented for giving her away. She also got to meet the little African boy who became a preacher and transformed his whole tribe. As the preacher took her to her mother's grave, he quoted these two scriptures:

"I tell you the truth, unless a kernel of wheat falls to the ground and dies, it remains only a single seed. But if it dies, it produces many seeds" (John 12:24, KJV).

"Those who sow in tears will reap with songs of joy" (Psalm 126:5, KJV).

This is the hope of His glory,that His children would live a holy abandoned life and their eyes would be fixed upon eternity. We live in an upside-down kingdom. Death is the door to life, and sorrow gives way to joy. The Bible emphatically states:

> So no wonder we don't give up. For even though our outer person gradually wears out, our inner being is renewed every single day. We view our slight, short-lived troubles in the light of eternity. We see our difficulties as the substance that produces for us an eternal, weighty glory far beyond all comparison, because we do not focus our attention on what is seen but on what is unseen. For what is seen is temporary, but the unseen realm is eternal.
>
> 2 Corinthians 4:16–18 (TPT)

I pray the words the Father has given me for this book have found their way into your story. I pray you have found the message of hope in *my* story of Hope. I remember the very first thing that awakened me out of my shock and trauma after Hope's passing. It was the singing of the birds. They never stopped singing when Hope took her last breath. They never stopped singing when I was trying to find mine again. I was drawn to them. Nothing had taken them by surprise or stopped them from making music. They continued on with what they were called to do. They had no worries about what tomorrow would bring, for it was all in the Father's hands.

> Look at the birds of the air, for they neither sow nor reap nor gather into barns; yet your heavenly Father feeds them. Are you not of more value than they? Which of you by worrying can add one cubit to his stature? "So why do you worry about clothing? Consider the lilies of the field, how they grow: they neither toil nor spin; and yet I say to you that even Solomon in all his glory was not arrayed like one of these. Now if God so clothes the grass of the field, which today is, and tomorrow is thrown into the oven, will He not much more clothe you, O you of little faith? "Therefore do not worry, saying, 'What shall we eat?' or 'What shall we drink?' or 'What shall we wear?' For after all these things the Gentiles seek. For your heavenly Father knows that you need all these things. But seek first the kingdom of God and His righteousness, and all these things shall be added to you. Therefore, do not worry about tomorrow, for tomorrow will worry about its own things. Sufficient for the day is its own trouble.
>
> Matthew 6:26–34 (NKJV)

Continue on, my friend. The Father knows what is needed in the hour of suffering. He can't be anything but good. He is there to fill every void, every hurt, every regret, every "why," and every painful memory with love and life. The cup of suffering may bring you to the edge of the Cliff of Abandonment, but only to gain the lenses of eternity through worship. The mountain before you will become a roadway to resurrection and hope. "And after you have suffered a little while, the God of all grace, who has called you to his eternal glory in Christ, will himself restore, confirm, strengthen, and establish you" (1 Peter 5:8–10, NKJV). May the goodness of the Father strengthen you as you suffer for only a little while. Wait on the Lord. "Wait for the Lord; be strong and take heart and wait for the Lord" (Psalm 27:14, NIV).

His song over you is Hope:

Even during the worst of days, in the worst of circumstances, His will for you is good and not evil.
His goodness is the only thing that will rescue you from the deepest pit of despair.
I declare over your hope.
Hope to breathe when it feels like you cannot anymore.
Hope to walk when it feels like you cannot even crawl.
Hope to hear what the Father is speaking louder than the lies of your enemy.
Hope to love and be loved.
Hope to laugh again.
Hope to find beauty in each day.
Hope to find the purpose that goes beyond the hour or moment.
Hope to cry.
Hope to laugh.
Hope to dream.
Hope to exhale.
Hope to stand.
Hope to wait.
Hope to see…
Hope that the Father will complete that which He began in you, now and throughout eternity. Find hope in your forward. In the sun that rises, in the birds that sing, in the laughter of a child, live in hope. Live in Jesus.

Now may God, the inspiration and fountain of hope, fill you to overflowing with uncontainable joy and perfect peace as you trust in him. And may the power of the Holy Spirit continually surround your life with his super-abundance until you radiate with hope!

Romans 15:13 (TPT)

Our story grabs the attention of every student we have the opportunity to share it with, and this open door has enabled us to be silence breakers, addressing the weapons Satan has used in the dark halls of shame and guilt, especially within the body of Christ. Help starts with a cry. It is our mandate to initiate that cry for help through the power of the Holy Spirit and our testimony of tragedy and hope.

"Not only so, but we also glory in our sufferings because we know that suffering produces perseverance; perseverance, character; and character, hope. And hope does not put us to shame, because God's love has been poured out into our hearts through the Holy Spirit, who has been given to us" (Romans 5:3–5). Pain and suffering will affect everyone, and our youth and young adults are certainly not void of it, especially as the world continues to get dark. It is our heart to teach a generation how to suffer well so that they might find hope at the end of their suffering.

Suffering well means to not just survive, but to thrive. It means to suffer in such a way that you become better and not bitter. In the midst of pain, you learn to find life, joy, and even purpose. You become an overcomer because you learn to walk out your pain inside the one who overcame it all for you, Jesus. This generation has been coined "Hopeless and lonely," but where Satan has brought hopelessness, Jesus is bringing Hope and resurrection power!

Family Ministry

A Generation Hurting

invite us to share in your youth Ministry www.chosenstones.org

Hope Noelle White
2002-2020

There is Hope Initiative

Using Hope's own journal's, writings, and our story of tragedy to healing, we are becoming a voice of Hope to her generation and beyond. Our heart is to minister to the broken hearted, to bereaved parents, to those who have suffered traumatic loss, to parents who are fighting for a son or daughter who is suffering with suicidal thoughts and depression, and to a generation of youth and young adults who suffer with low self-esteem, not knowing their identity in Christ, and suicidal and self-harm tendencies.

Breaking the Silence

Breaking the power of the Spirit of Suicide

Our story grabs the attention of every student we have the opportunity to share it with, and this open door has enabled us to be silence breakers, addressing the weapons Satan has used in the dark halls of shame and guilt, especially within the body of Christ. Help starts with a cry. It is our mandate to initiate that cry for help through the power of the Holy Spirit and our testimony of tragedy and hope.

Testimony:

"I am so grateful that Kylie and I could attend last night. There aren't the right words to articulate all the emotions I felt leaving last evening. The anointing and presence of God were so powerful. Thank you from the bottom of my heart for being so vulnerable in sharing your loss and pain to reach so many in need. Hope's story and testimony are bringing life, restoration and healing to a generation in such need. Hell is losing its grip on our teens, and I believe many teens were set free last night. God bless you always, Alicia."

I have reserved the last few pages to honor our sweet Hope. She is beholding the one in which she knew, talked about, and drew about.

Hope on a Mission trip to Mexico

Hope's journal page that has now become our logo for the "There Is Hope" initiative

Painting brought Hope peace.

Hope's painting, *The Garden*

Hope's painting, *Blooming*